ORIGIN

OF

THE PINDARIES

ORIGIN

OF

THE PINDARIES;

PRECEDED BY

HISTORICAL NOTICES

ON

THE RISE

OF THE

DIFFERENT MAHRATTA STATES.

BY JOHN CLUNES

(OFFICER, THE HONOURABLE EAST INDIA COMPANY)

GYAN

Published by

GYAN

Gyan Publishing House
5, Ansari Road
Daryaganj, New Delhi-110002
Phone: 011-47034999, 9811692060
E-mail: books@gyanbooks.com

Distribution Network
gyanbooks.com
India, USA, Canada, UK, Australia

ISBN: 978-81-212-6458-7 (PB)
First Published, 1818

2nd Impression 2024

Printed at: Gyan Press, Delhi.

ORIGIN OF THE PINDARIES
Author: JOHN CLUNES

ORIGIN

OF

THE PINDARIES;

PRECEDED BY

HISTORICAL NOTICES

ON

THE RISE

OF THE

DIFFERENT MAHRATTA STATES.

BY AN OFFICER,

IN THE SERVICE OF

THE HONOURABLE EAST INDIA COMPANY.

Ipsam coloniam invasere, nec ullum in barbaris sævitiæ genus omisit ira et victoria. C. CORN. TACITI AGRICOLA.

LONDON:

JOHN MURRAY, ALBEMARLE-STREET.

1818.

INTRODUCTION.

AN Officer, in the Service of the East-India Company, offers the following summary of the Mahratta History to the Public, because there does not, to his knowledge, exist, any regular or connected account of this singular people; and because at such a juncture as the present, when the repeated aggressions of predatory horse, have again compelled the British Government to take arms, any information, however trifling and imperfect, cannot but prove acceptable to those who are interested in the welfare and prosperity of the Company's possessions in the East. A considerable part of the work has been composed from manuscript documents, from the personal inquiries and observations of the author, who, during a residence of many years in India, has had frequent opportunities of becoming acquainted with the political situation of the country; and from the communications of many able and intelligent friends, whose names he does not feel himself at liberty to mention, but to whom he takes this opportunity of acknowledging his obligations. The printed authorities which have been referred to, are chiefly the India Papers submitted to Parliament, relative to the late Mahratta Wars; Scott's Translation of Ferishta, Malcolm's Political Sketch, Wilkes's South of India, the Asiatic Researches, and Asiatic Annual Registers.

SKETCH

OF THE

MAHRATTA HISTORY,

&c. &c

CHAP. I.

THE origin of the family of Suttarah, like that of many others, who have risen to fame and greatness, is lost in the mists of fable and tradition. By some they are stated to be derived from the obscure Potail of a paltry village in the Pergunnah of Poonah; whilst, by others, they are said to boast an illegitimate descent from the Rajahs of Oudipoor* and Cheitore, the most ancient of the Hindoo Princes of India. Be that as it may, the immediate founder of the family

* The family of Oudipoor is mentioned by Ptolemy, and said to be as ancient as the rocks of Ajmere. Their usual place of residence was Cheitore, a celebrated fortress and city, which stood several sieges against the Mahomedans, but was at last taken and destroyed by Akbar.

would appear to have been a person named Baug Sing* Bhanslah†, who, after a variety of adventures in Malwa and Kandeish, purchased a small Zemindary to the S. of Poonah, where he built a castle, which he named Suttarah, from its seventeen towers‡. This person retained in his employ a band of desperate marauders, and commenced a system of depredation, which the feeble government of Beejepoor was unable to repress, and which his descendants have, although on a much larger scale, pursued ever since. Baug Sing died at an advanced age, and left a son named Maulojee, who entered the service of Jadao Row, a powerful Jagheerdar of the kingdom of Ahmednugger, under whom he acquired considerable wealth and reputation. Maulojee was the first who assumed the title of Rajah, and his fort of Suttarah, enriched with plunder, insensibly

---

* Ferishta.

† The mother of the founder of this family, is said to have been an obscure woman of the Mahratta tribe of Bhonslah, a name which was taken by her, and by which the Rajahs of Suttarah and Berar, are still distinguished.—*Indian Reports*.

‡ Others say it was named Suttarah from its shape, which resembled a star.—MSS.

swelled into a populous town*. Sahoojee, his eldest son, having married the daughter of Jadao Row, in opposition to the wishes of her parents, was compelled, after a desperate resistance, to fly from the fort of Mahooly†, where he had been besieged by his father-in-law. He was so closely pursued, that his wife, then seven months gone with child, and consequently unable to endure much fatigue, fell into the power of her father, who sent her to the fortress of Savanore, where, on the 17th of May, 1627, she gave birth to the celebrated Sevajee‡.

Sahoojee fled to Beejepoor, and sought an asylum with Ibrahim Adil Shah; and, being unable to procure the release of his wife and child, he married another lady, by whom he had a son named Eccojee§, who conquered Tanjore, and transmitted the conquest to his descendants. Sahoojee accompanied Rundoolla Khan, a distinguished Ameer in the service of Ibrahim Shah, upon

* MSS.

† See Wilkes's South of India.

‡ Ibid.

§ For the history of the Mahratta conquest of Tanjore, see Wilkes's distinguished work on the South of India.

an expedition into the Carnatic; and was afterwards intrusted with the government of the provinces, subject to the king of Beejepoor, in Mysore. His usual places of residence, were Bangalore and Colar*, but he still possessed his patrimony of Suttarah and Poonah, which he intrusted to the management of Dundejee Pundit†; with strict injunctions, to use no effort untried in order to procure the release of Sevajee and his mother. This old and faithful servant succeeded in accomplishing the wishes of his master, and educated the youth with the utmost care and attention, until he attained his seventeenth year, when the natural warmth and independence of his temper, led him to despise the instructions of his guardian‡. Sevajee, fired with the example of his forefathers, and taking advantage of the inefficiency of the government of Beejepoor, placed himself at the head of an armed banditti, and ravaged with impunity

---

* A small town in Mysore, and the birth-place of Hyder Ali Khan.

† Scott's Translation of Ferishta.

‡ See Wilkes.

the western parts of the Deckan. His boldness and activity, added to his fame and his riches, enabled him to increase the number of his followers. He became, in the course of a few years, the terror of the neighbouring countries, and was commonly known by the appellation of Sevajee the Robber*. His ravages, at last, roused the slumbering court of Beejepoor, and occasioned the recall of his father, who was summoned from Mysore to repress the turbulence of his son. But there is reason to believe, that Sahoojee secretly abetted and rejoiced at the daring enterprises of Sevajee, whose rising fortunes he foresaw, and whom he invited to Poonah, where he was received with royal honours†.

The convulsed state of the Mogul empire, opened a noble field to the fierce and aspiring

---

* Wilkes, and MSS.

† Sahoojee was, in consequence, imprisoned on his return to Beejepoor; and only escaped an ignominious death by the powerful intercession of Rund oolla Khan, who had always been his friend and patron. He was permitted to return to his government of the Carnatic Balaghaut, and was killed, in 1667, by a fall from his horse in hunting, at Bednore, where a tomb was erected to his memory, by Rund oolla Khan.—*Ferishta*.

genius of Sevajee, who, from the captain of a band of robbers, became sovereign of a country, which at the time of his death, extended along the western coast of India, from Soonda to Guzzerat. When Aurengzebe first came into the Deckan, Sevajee appeared at his court and made a proffer of his services, which were accepted*. He accompanied the Mogul army to Golcondah†, and acquitted himself so much to the satisfaction of the prince, that he was permitted to collect the choute, or a fourth part of the revenues of Telingana‡: but, on the departure of Aurengzebe to Delhi, Sevajee disdaining the condition of a sub-

---

* MSS., and Historical Narrative of the Mahratta State.

† An ancient city and fortress in the Deckan, situated about six miles from Hyderabad. It was the capital of the Bhamane and Cutulo Shahee Dynasties, and was taken by Aurengzebe, after a siege of seven months, in 1690. The treasures of the Nizam are now deposited at Golcondah, and no European is permitted to enter that fortress, without the express permission of his Highness.

‡ A very ancient Hindoo kingdom, including Berar and the Eastern part of the Deckan, of which Warangole, a city now in ruins, was the capital. These ruins are said to extend six or seven miles in length, and to consist of a great number of Pagodas and decayed Choultries, scattered at a distance from each other, in the midst of a jungle.

ject, boldly threw off his allegiance, and erected the standard of revolt. He levied heavy contributions, with merciless indiscrimination, on all the provinces which he did not reduce to submission; made a treaty with the unfortunate Tannah Shah, king of Golcondah, whom he immediately afterwards betrayed, and invading the Carnatic, took the strong forts of Ginjee* and Vellore†. He compelled his brother Eccojee‡ to seek refuge in his capital of Tanjore; and having reduced all the country to the north of the Coleroon§, returned through Mysore to Suttarah with immense booty. The latter part of his life was spent in a perpetual struggle with Aurengzebe, who wrested from

---

* An ancient town and fortress in the Carnatic, said to have been founded by the Chola kings, 37 miles N.W. from Pondicherry. The fort occupies the summit of a high rock; it has stood several sieges, but is now neglected and in ruins, in consequence of the unhealthiness of the climate.

† A town and fortress in the Carnatic, 88 miles W. by S. of Madras.

‡ See Wilkes's South of India.

§ The Coleroon is the northern branch of the river Caverry, which, after a course of about eighty miles, falls into the sea, at Dericotta. The greater part of it is absorbed in the cultivation of the land.

him a great part of his conquests*, and forced him to retire to his strong holds amongst the mountains of the Conkan†, where he died in 1680.

He was succeeded by his son Sambajee, who inheriting the spirit and ambition of his father‡, continued the contest with Aureng-

---

* In 1664, Sevajee, unable to defend himself in the fortress of Poorunder, threw himself upon the mercy of Aurengzebe, and went to Delhi; but, entertaining fears for his personal security, he effected his escape in a bread-basket, from the house in which he was confined, and after undergoing much fatigue, returned to the Conkan, and in a short time recovered his former power. His death, according to Ferishta, was occasioned by the curses of a Mahomedan Saint, whom he had insulted. The Mahrattas, however, imagine that he was poisoned by his wife.—*Scott's Ferishta.*

† The country which runs between the western Ghauts and the sea, from the province of Canara to Guzzerat. It may be termed an inclined plain, about thirty or forty miles in width, gradually sloping from the foot of the mountains to the sea, and is a fertile country, intersected by many small rivers. Raree and Ryeghur, both favourite residences of Sevajee, may be considered as the strongest fortresses in the Conkan. The former now belongs to the Rajah of Colapore, and is situated on the sea coast, seventeen miles N. of Goa.

‡ Ferishta says, that Sambajee possessed no talents for government, and that he was entirely devoted to wine and

zebe, by whom he was taken, and put to death in 1691. Sahoojee, the son of Sambajee, was the third Rajah of Sattarah, and under this prince the Mahratta power approached toward its zenith. It is probable, however, that the conduct of Aurengzebe himself, in annihilating the Mahomedan kings of the Deckan, who alone could offer any opposition to the arms of Sahoojee, contributed more towards the conquests and aggrandizement of the Mahrattas, than even the example of Sevajee, or the valour of his followers. The wars which the emperor waged with his brothers, required the constant presence of himself and his army in Hindostan; and, as he was unable or unwilling to employ the disbanded troops, and numerous retainers of the governments, which he had destroyed, they thronged in numbers to the assistance of the invaders*. The majo-

---

women; whilst on the contrary the Mahrattas assert, that he was a prince of great courage and enterprise. He was surprised by the troops of Aurengzebe near Pernalla, a celebrated fort in the province of Beejepoor, and had a hot iron drawn over his eyes previous to his execution.

* Zoolfukar Khan, according to Ferishta, defeated the Mahrattas no less than nineteen times in the course of six

rity of these men were of Mahratta descent, and although the name had long been lost in oblivion, they continued to speak the same language, and naturally preferred the service

---

months. Our author ascribes as a reason for the rapid rise of these plunderers, that the government of the provinces was formerly confided to Omrahs of great rank, who always maintained in their employ, a large body of troops; but that it was afterwards held by nobles of inferior rank, poor, and rapacious, who, while they neglected to support the usual force, were at the same time guilty of great injustice and oppression. The authority of government consequently sunk, the Zemindars broke into rebellion, and the Foujdars, destitute of troops, and therefore unable to command obedience, entered into secret engagements with refractory chiefs, which only tended to render them more insolent. The Zemindars were deprived of their arms by order of the Emperor; and being left a prey to the followers of Sevajee, were, in self-defence, compelled to join the standard of the invaders. Contributions were therefore exacted instead of settled revenues, the satellites of the court were guilty of the most shameful abuses; and a capitation tax levied with unrelenting severity on the Hindoos, created universal disgust amongst that class of men. The ryots, thus oppressed by the imperialists, abandoned their farms in despair, and in their turn became plunderers for want of employment. It is curious to trace the striking resemblance between this description, and the system which now pervades the Asiatic provinces of Turkey: or, to approach nearer home, the territories of our ally, his highness the Nizam.

of a prince of their own religion * to that of the Mahomedans, by whom they were in general oppressed or despised. The roving life of a freebooter was besides better suited to the inclinations of the idle and ambitious, who swarmed in every province of the Deckan.

Soon after Sahoojee's † accession to the musnud, it became apparent that he was naturally of a pacific disposition ; and it was this which ultimately led to the usurpation of the supreme authority by Bajeerow Bishwanut ‡, who, with the title of Peishwah or Prudhaun, assumed the entire management of public affairs. Bajeerow was a person of

* Mahrastra was an ancient Hindoo kingdom, extending along the coast of Malabar, from the mouths of the Sapti to Goa.

† Jadao Row, or, as he is called by Scott, Dhunnah Jadao, distinguished himself in the Mahratta wars, against the generals of Aurengzebe in the beginning of Sahoojee's reign ; but even at this time divisions prevailed among the Mahratta chiefs, and Jadao Row is represented as having acted to a certain degree independently of the Rajah of Suttarah. The Pindaries are frequently mentioned in these wars, and in particular the chief, named Ponnapah, who resided at Kerah, and who afterwards, driven from hence, ravaged part of the Carnatic, and took Vellore.

‡ Ballajeerow, the father of Bajeerow, was a Bramin of Suwurdun in the Conkan, and commanded five hundred horse in the service of Sevajee.

great ability, and his wisdom and policy continued to his family the power which he had originally usurped: this form of government has subsisted until the present day, the title is become hereditary, and on the death of a Peishwah, his successor is invested by his now titular sovereign with the ensigns of office*. The name of the Rajah of Suttarah is in fact almost forgotten, and the Peishwah being in the possession of the executive power and authority, has been invariably treated as the legitimate head of the Mahratta empire †.

The death of Aurengzebe which occurred in 1707, and the civil wars which distracted the Mogul Empire ever afterwards, stimulated the Mahrattas to exertion, and presented to the Peishwah, an admirable opportunity for carrying his ambitious schemes into execution. At a meeting of the principal chiefs convened by Bajeerow before he took the field, it was agreed that each chieftain should maintain a certain number of troops, and keeping one-half of the spoil taken by himself, should

---

* See Papers relative to the late Mahratta War laid before Parliament.

† India Reports and MSS.

deliver the other to the Peishwah or rather to his master, the Rajah of Suttarah *. This convention gave rise to the Mahratta confederacy, and changed the nature of the government from an absolute monarchy, as it existed under Sevajee, to a sort of republic of chieftains, who were guaranteed in the possession of certain rights and privileges, and permitted to govern their own Jagheers in any manner they thought proper, on condition that they should recognise Sahoojee as the head of the empire, and the Peishwah as his prime minister †.

Bajeerow commenced his operations by the taking of Beejepoor, and by levying the choute on the districts around Hyderabad. All the open country lying between the Nerbudda ‡ and the Toombudra § submitted to

---

* MSS.

† MSS.

‡ One of the finest rivers in India, it has its source in the province of Gundwana; and after pursuing a westerly course of nearly seven hundred miles, empties itself into the Gulf of Cambay, near Baroach. The Nerbudda divides the Deckan from Hindostan, and is not fordable for many months in the year.

§ A large river which divides the territories of the Company from those of the Nizam. It is formed by the junction

him; and he subsequently took a leading part in the disputes between the sons of Bahader Shah, and was invited to Delhi at the head of an army *. On the deposition of Ferocksere in 1719, and the succession of Mahomed Shah Allum, Ali Khan, was appointed soubahdar of the Deckan, and Bajeerow who was then at the capital, was requested to install him in his new office. But previously to his departure from the court, the crafty Mahratta demanded, as a remuneration for past services, permission to collect the choute from the provinces of Bengal, Malwa † and Guzzerat. The feeble representative of Timour had not the power of refusing this insolent demand, and his compliance therewith materially contributed towards the fu-

---

of the Tunga and Bhudra, both of which have their sources in the western Ghauts, about the parallel of Mangalore. This river which falls into the Kistna, between the 78th and 79th degrees of east longitude, contains a large volume of water during the S. W. Monsoon, but is fordable in the dry seasons.

* Historical Narrative.

† A large province of Hindostan, extending along the northern bank of the Nerbudda, nearly three hundred miles in length, and about one hundred and fifty in breadth. It is a mountainous, but rich, fertile, and well-watered country, capable of producing abundance of the finest cotton.

ture aggrandizement of the Mahrattas, inasmuch as it paved the way to the subjugation of some of the most fertile provinces of the Mogul empire, and gave Bajeerow a legitimate right to interfere in the affairs of Hindostan *. Allum Ali Khan had scarcely been seated in his government, before he was called upon to oppose the famous Nizam ool' Moolk, by whom he was defeated and slain near Ballapore †. Bajeerow, on the promise of an additional choute, joined his forces to those of the successful Soubahdar; and turning every occurrence to his own advantage, followed up his plans with unwearied perseverance ‡.

In 1724 Guzzerat was subdued by Pillajee Guickwar, who, fixing his residence at Broderah §, was permitted by Sahoojee to assume the title of Rajah, which his successors still retain; and, in 1732, the Peish-

---

* Historical Narrative of the Mahratta State.

† Ballapore is a small town in Berar, about thirty miles from Ellichpoor.—MSS.

‡ Historical Narrative.

§ A city and fortress in Guzzerat, situate in lat. 22° 13′ N. long. 73° 24′ E. It is a large and flourishing town, and the usual residence of the Guickwar, or Mahratta Chief, of Guzzerat.—*Scott's Ferishta*.

wah procured for himself the title of Soubahdar* of Malwa †, the whole of which province, together with the greater part of Kandeish ‡, he had already reduced.

In 1735 he invaded Bundelcund §, whilst Mulhar Row Holkar overran the provinces of Agra ||, and carried his devastations to the

* Scott's Ferishta.

† This province was at first divided between the Rājah of Suttarah, the Peishwah, and Mulhar Row Holkar; but Bajeerow afterwards gave his master's share to Janajee Scindiah, the ancestor of Dowlut Row.

‡ An ancient Soubah of the Deckan, about one hundred and eighty miles in length, and eighty in breadth. It is situated to the S. of Malwa, and abounds in strong castles. It is partly possessed by the Peishwah, partly by the Holkar family, and partly by Scindiah, who always keeps a garrison in Asseerghur, the strongest fortress in the province.

§ An extensive and mountainous province of Hindostan, situate between the 24th and 26th degrees of north latitude. This province, when ceded to the British Government, was in a neglected state, being in a great measure covered with jungle, but its geographical position, as immediately adjoining the territories of the predatory powers, could not fail to make it, in a political point of view, a highly valuable acquisition.

|| The capital of a province of the same name in Hindostan, situate on the right bank of the Jumna, and the capital of the Mogul empire in the reign of Akbar. It is one hundred and thirty-seven miles from Delhi, and about eight hundred from Calcutta.

gates of that city. Holkar was defeated, however, by Boorhan ool Moolk, and after losing half of his army in the Jumna, he joined the Peishwah under the walls of Gwalior. Bajeerow then advanced to Delhi, carrying fire and desolation into that devoted country, and was only induced to retire in consequence of the advance of Boorhan ool Moolk, and a promise from Mahomed of the choute of the whole of the Mogul empire*. He returned to Malwa, where he remained until 1738, when Nizam ool Moolk having proceeded to Delhi, to meet Nadir Shah, Bajeerow conceived that the absence of the father offered a fair occasion for effecting the destruction of the son, and accordingly advanced to Aurungabad†, against Nazir Jung, who had been left in charge of the government. The young prince by no means intimidated, put himself at the head of his army, and forced

*. Scott's Ferishta.

† A large city, and once the capital of the Deckan, but now fallen to decay. It is situated a few miles from Dowletabad, and contains the ruins of a palace, said to have been built by Aurengzebe, when he laid siege to that fortress.

the Mahrattas to retire. The armies afterwards came in sight of each other, near Poonah, and the issue of a desperate action fought in the plains to the north-east of that city, was fatal to Bajeerow, and glorious to Nazir Jung; who, after having burnt Poonah, and the Pettah of Suttarah, returned in triumph to Aurungabad *. Bajeerow died a few months after his defeat, and his son, Ballajee Row, was immediately afterwards invested by Sahoojee with the title of Peishwah, and with the whole of the authority annexed to the situation †. Ballajee Row was not inferior to his father in courage, talents, or ambition; and under his directions the power of the Mahrattas was felt from the Sutlege ‡ to the Caverry, and from the Gulf of Cambay to the shores of Cuttack.

Sahoojee died in 1740, in the fiftieth year of his reign §, during the greater part of which time he had scarcely ever moved

---

* Historical Narrative, and MSS.

† Historical Narrative.

‡ The ancient Hyphasis, and one of the rivers of the Punjab.

§ India Reports, and MSS.

beyond the threshold of his palace at Suttarah. His name had, indeed, been almost forgotten during the latter years of his life. He insensibly became an empty pageant, and although his successors continue to be treated with the outward marks of sovereignty *, they cannot be viewed in any other light, than as the state prisoners of the Peishwah †. It would seem as if the extraordinary exertions of Sevajee had exhausted the vital heat of the blood, since none of his descendants, excepting Sambajee, displayed a single spark of his spirit, or made the smallest effort to recover that authority, of which they had tamely suffered themselves to be deprived. Sahoojee having no children of his own, had adopted his grand-nephew, Madajee Bhonslah, but this person was deemed unfit to fill the situation of Rajah of Suttarah, and the selection

* No Peishwah can enter upon the duties of his office without receiving a dress of honour from the Rajah of Suttarah. The country round his residence is exempt from taxation; and when a chief enters the district of Suttarah the ensigns of power are laid aside, and the nakaru ceases to beat.—*India Papers.*

† India Papers.

fell on Ram Rajah, a prince of weak understanding, and of a disposition still more feeble and indolent than that of his predecessor *. He was consequently a fit tool for the purposes of Ballajee Row, by whom, indeed, he had been raised to the musnud †. The abilities and exertions of the new Peishwah, together with the precipitate conduct of Nazir Jung, and the want of union on the part of their enemies, soon enabled the Mahrattas to retrieve their affairs, and to wipe away the disgrace of their defeat at Poonah.

About 1741 Ragojee Bhonslah, the buckshee, or commander-in-chief of the troops, conquered Berar, and part of Gundwana ‡, these provinces were at first granted to him in jagheer, and afterwards erected by him into an independent principality, which he governed

---

* MSS.

† MSS.

‡ A large province belonging to the Rajah of Berar, extending from the 19th to the 25th degree of north latitude, bounded on the E. by Bengal and Orissa, and on the W. by Berar. The far greater proportion of this province is poor, uncultivated, covered with jungle, and yielding but a slender revenue to its possessor, the Rajah of Berar.

under the title of Rajah of Berar*. He established himself at Nagpore, in Gundwana, then an insignificant village, and as he considered Ballajee Row as his rival, and the usurper of his rights, he seldom acted in unison with him †. This year Morari Row, one of the generals of the Peishwah, having penetrated into the Carnatic, took Trichinopoly, and was appointed governor of the countries to the north of the Coleroon, which he oppressed for upwards of two years, when he was expelled by Nizam ool Moolk, and obtained a permanent cession of the district and fortress of Gooti ‡.

The Peishwah did not fail to avail himself of the death of Nizam ool Moolk (who died at Boorhanpoor§ on the 24th of March,

---

* India Papers, and MSS.

† MSS.

‡ The capital of a district of the same name in the ceded provinces, situated in lat. 59° 9′ N., long. 77° 35′ E. The fortress, which is situated on a hill, was taken by Morari Row from the Nabob of Savanore, in 1758. It remained in the possession of the Mahrattas about twenty years, and was ceded by the Nizam to the Company in 1800.—*See Wilkes and Orme.*

§ The ancient capital of Candeish, situated on the banks of the Tapti, about one hundred and fifty miles from

1748), and of the departure of Nazir Jung to the Carnatic, to foment the jealousy already subsisting between the sons of the late Soubahdar, with the view of reaping the harvest of their quarrels *. This was a game which he played from the beginning to the termination of his career, with equal constancy and success, and with all that villany and habitual duplicity so peculiar to his tribe. Alternately presenting himself as the protector or avenger of one or other of the princes, he levied contributions at the gates of Aurungabad and Boorhanpoor, entered Hindostan, and obtained a cession of several fertile districts in the provinces of Agra and Allahabad †. Salabut Jung, who

---

Oujein. It was once a large and magnificent city, but is now, for the greater part, in ruins.

* Historical Narrative.

† The most distinguished of his coadjutors were his brothers, Chimnajee, Ragonaut Row, and Sedasheo Bhow, together with Junkoo, Mulhar Row, Holkar, and Janajee Scindiah. The two latter possessed extensive lands in Malwa and Candeish, whence they made constant irruptions into the territories of the Rajpoot princes of Ajmere. Scindiah's usual place of residence was the ancient city of Oujein, in Malwa; and Holkar established his capital at Indore, thirty miles W. of the former city. In 1750 Jana-

had succeeded his brother as Soubahdar of the Deckan, exasperated at the treachery and rapacity of Ballajee Row, took the field against him at the head of a numerous and well-appointed army *, with several battalions disciplined in the European manner, commanded by the famous Marquis de Bussy; but the Peishwah, unable openly to face such an army, contented himself with laying waste the country, and with harassing the troops of the Nizam, by unremitted attacks on his flanks and rear, a system of warfare generally adopted by the Mahrattas, whose armies consisted of irregular horse. Poonah was again abandoned to the flames,

---

jee Scindiah marched with an army to Delhi, to support Ghazee ood deen Khan (the eldest son of Nizam ool Moolk), with whom he returned to Aurungabad some months afterwards. Here Ghazee ood deen Khan perished in an attempt to recover the possession of the Deckan, from his younger brother Salabat Jung; but his son, who took the name and titles of his father, and who afterwards played a distinguished part in the revolutions at Delhi, still maintained a large body of Mahrattas in his service. They accompanied him in his expedition against Ahmed Shah, whose camp they surprised and plundered.

* Historical Narrative.

but Salabat Jung was ultimately driven back into his own dominions *.

In 1751, Morari Row of Gooti, was invited by the contending powers of the French and English †, once more to enter the Carnatic ‡: and in 1752 the Peishwah opened the campaign against the Nizam at the head of fifty thousand § horse, gave him battle in the vicinity of Bedur ‖, and compelled him to sign a treaty, whereby Salabut Jung agreed to give in exchange for certain districts in the neighbourhood of Aurungabad others more valuable, bordering upon Boorhanpoor, the favourite residence of Nizam ool Moolk ¶. Ballajee Row then proceeded to ravage the frontiers of Mysore, while Ragojee Bhonslah prosecuted his conquests to the N.E. of Berar.

---

* MSS.

† MSS.

‡ He remained there upwards of two years, at the end of which period he returned to his jagheer, laden with spoil.

§ MSS.

‖ The capital of a province of the same name in the Deckan. It is a large but ruinous town, was formerly the residence of the Rhamanee kings, and is situate in 17° 47′ north lat. 77° 48′ east.

¶ MSS.

Scarcely a month now passed without some movement or irruption of the Mahrattas* who had insinuated themselves into every part of the Mogul Empire ; and like a swarm of devouring locusts preyed upon the fruits of the land. Ballajee Row broke into Mysore, invested Seringapatam and Bangalore, took Sera † and Cuddapah ‡, and was induced to return, by the payment of thirty-two lacks of rupees §.

Whilst these transactions took place under the management of the Peishwah, another army commanded by Ragonath Row, Scindiah Junkoo, and Mulhar Row Holkar, accompanied the young Ghazee ood deen Khan to Delhi, and became the principal actors in

---

* In 1753 Orissa was ceded to the Berar Mahrattas by Aliverdy Khan, who was also compelled, for a short time, to pay them the choute from Bengal and Bahar.

† A town in Mysore, about eighty miles N. of Seringapatam.

‡ The capital of a district in the ceded provinces, formerly the residence of an independent race of Pattan princes. It is one hundred and fifty-three miles from Madras, and two hundred and thirty from Hyderabad.

§ In this campaign the Peishwah was opposed by the famous Hyder Ali Khan, who then commanded the Mysore army.—*See Wilkes.*

the revolutions and cruelties which deluged that capital in blood. They obtained large possessions in Lahore*, which first brought them in contact with the Afgans, who, in 1759, drove Junkoo from Lahore, and beat Scindiah not far from Delhi. Holkar, then at Jyepoor †, advanced to the support of his friends, but he was also defeated with great slaughter at Secundra ‡, twenty coss E. of Delhi §. These events closed the year 1759, and in 1760, a war broke out between the Peishwah and Nizam Ali Khan, who had

* A celebrated city in a province of the same name, situated on the left bank of the Ravery, lat. 31° 50′ N., long. 73° 48′ E. It is now the residence of Runjeet Sing, chief of the Seiks, but is fallen from its ancient grandeur, although still a town of considerable consequence.

† Or, as it is more commonly called, Jyenagur, is a rich tract of country, extending along the right bank of the Jumna, about one hundred and fifty miles long from north to south, and seventy in width from east to west. It is governed by a Rajpoot prince, who styles himself the Rajah of Jyepoor, and resides at a town of the same name, situated in lat. 26° 56′ N. long. 75° 40′ E. This province is rich and fertile, but has long been subject to the ravages of the Mahrattas.

‡ A town in Hindostan, twenty-eight miles S. E. of Delhi.

§ See Scott and MSS.

assumed the management of affairs in the Deckan. The result of a battle fought* on the banks of the Poonah †, reduced the Nizam to the necessity of sueing for peace, which was granted him on the humiliating terms of ceding to the Peishwah the impregnable fortress of Dowlutabad ‡, Asseerghur §, and the provinces of Boornapoor and Candeish, countries yielding an annual revenue of sixty lacks of rupees ||. Ballajee Row in this war had meditated the entire conquest of the Deckan, and regarding M. de Bussy as the chief obstacle of the completion of his views, had offered him a magnificent esta-

---

* Historical Narrative.

† A river in the Deckan, which has its source in the Injardy hills, from whence it flows west through the province of Berar, and falls into the Tapti, about twenty miles below Boorhanpoor.—*Hamilton.*

‡ Dowlutabad, or Deoghur, a very ancient and celebrated town and fortress in the Deckan, situate in lat. 19° 52′ N., long. 76° 2′ E. This fortress crowns the summit of a mountain, and is deemed impregnable by the natives.

§ A very strong fort, now belonging to Scindiah, in the province of Candeish. It was ceded to Madajee Scindiah by the Poonah government, and taken by Colonel Stevenson in the last Mahratta war.

|| MSS.

blishment to enter the Mahratta service. But this distinguished officer having rejected the offer *, the Peishwah entered into a negotiation with the English, who promised to assist him with a small corps for the purpose of expelling the French from the Nizam's dominions. These troops had, however, no sooner arrived from England, than he employed them in reducing Angria to submission, with the view of making himself master of the immense wealth which that pirate had accumulated, but which, to his great mortification, fell into the hands of the captors.

Soon after the conclusion of the above treaty with Nizam Ali Khan, the Peishwah despatched his brother Sedasheo Row, commonly called the Bhow, and his son Biswoss Row, a youth of sixteen years of age, in command of the largest army he had ever sent into the field, to retrieve the losses which had been sustained in the northern parts of Hindostan, by the defeats of Scindiah and Holkar. The Bhow reached Delhi without much opposition, and compelled the Afgan governor to capitulate. But he

* MSS.

had no sooner entered the city, than he began to kill and plunder the defenceless inhabitants, and he caused the silver sheathing to be torn from the ceiling of the imperial Dewan Khana*, for the purpose of being melted into coin. He placed Shah Jehan Buksh upon the throne, appointed Naroo Sunker to the command of the garrison, and quitted the city to oppose Ahmed Shah, king of Cabul, laden with spoil and with the imprecations of the natives†. But his bad conduct and indecision shewed that his abilities were unequal to the trust that had been reposed in him. Instead of keeping the field with his horse, according to the customs of his country, and continually hovering round the enemy, without risking a decisive battle, he injudiciously shut himself up in a fortified camp, near the town of Paniput; where, after his men had become dispirited, and his horses nearly famished, he

---

* See Scott.

† The rapid strides which the Mahrattas were daily making towards power, and the threatened extermination of every Mahomedan government in India, is said to have induced Ahmed Shah to advance from Cabul, in defence of the faithful.

was forced to fight on the most disadvantageous terms. The result of such a battle could not for an instant be doubtful; his army, whatever may be said of their desperate courage on that day, did not combat for victory but safety, and a retreat was all that they were anxious to secure*. The slaughter was consequently immense, and the defeat most complete: three hundred thousand † men, the gene-

* Cassi Rajah Pundit says, that the whole Mahratta army, as if by enchantment, turned their backs and fled, leaving the field of battle covered with heaps of the slain. The victors gave no quarter, and the pursuit continued for ten or twelve coss in every direction in which they fled.—*See the 3d vol. of the Asiatic Researches.*

† According to Cassi Rajah Pundit there were about five hundred thousand souls in the Mahratta camp, of whom the greater part were killed or taken prisoners; and of those who escaped from the field of battle and the pursuit, many were destroyed by the Zemindars of the country. The plunder was immense, and our author says, that a single horseman might be observed carrying off eight or ten camels, laden with valuable effects. Sedasheo Row was thought to have been killed, but in the year 1779, a person appeared at Benares who called himself the Bhow, and stated that, though wounded, he had escaped from the battle, and fled to the hills of Cumaoon, where he had resided for several years. He produced many circumstantial proofs that he was the Bhow; his age, person, and several marks about his body strongly supported that belief, although there

ral, and every chief excepting Holkar, are said to have fallen in this sanguinary combat*, or in the pursuit; the flower of the Mahratta youth was swept away, and had the Mahomedans followed up the blow, the star of the house of Sevajee would probably have set for ever†.

The battle of Paniput, perhaps the most bloody recorded in history, was fought in the month of January, 1761, and it still forms an epocha in the annals of Hindostan. This signal defeat spread a general gloom and awful stillness over the Mahratta states, which, for sixty years, had been the scene of a constant and restless activity; and the Peishwah was so much affected by the death of his son and brother, and by the threatened misfortunes of his family, that he soon afterwards died of a broken heart‡.

---

appeared a difference in temper and manner, which excited doubt. His history was investigated both by Mr. Graham and Mr. Hastings, but he was suffered to linger in confinement until 1781, when he was set at liberty, but soon after died.—*See the 3d vol. of the Asiatic Researches.*

* Ferishta says that Holkar and two other chiefs escaped. Janajee Scindiah was taken alive, but afterwards put to death.

† See Scott's Ferishta.

‡ MSS.

From this period the Mahratta princes seldom acted in unison, the extent of their conquests, together with the conditions under which they were achieved, having, as I have already observed, changed the form of the government from a monarchy to that of a confederacy of chiefs*, henceforward intent

* The most distinguished families are those of Suttarah, Berar, and Colapore, (derived from the same stock), Holkar, Scindiah, and Guickwar, most of whom have risen to sovereignty since the days of Sevajee.

The first, Ragojee Bhonslah, died in 1749, and was succeeded by his son Janajee; who, dying in 1772, left his dominions to Ragojee Bhonslah his nephew, being the son of his younger brother, Madajee Bhonslah. This occasioned a contention between Janajee's brothers, Sahojee and Madajee, (the former claiming the government by right of birth, and the latter as the father and guardian of the adopted child), which terminated in the death of Sahoojee, who was killed in action, in January 1795. Madajee Bhonslah governed Berar, as guardian of his son, till 1788, when he died at an advanced age, and was succeeded by his son, the late Rajah Ragojee Bhonslah. This prince died in March, 1816, and was succeeded by his son Pursajee, the present Rajah, whose imbecility had led to the elevation of his cousin Appah Sahib to the situation of Dewan. The Rajah of Berar never considered himself as subordinate to the Peishwah; on occasions of ceremony, he is treated as the superior in rank, and, as the first prince of the empire, claims the right of sending the Peishwah a Khelaut on his

on individual schemes of ambition, which were promoted by the turbulent and unsettled state of the times. The descendants of

---

accession to office. He also claims the privilege of being consulted, before the conclusion of any alliance between the Peishwah and any other state. These pretensions have, however, never been admitted, and Ragojee Bhonslah has either been considered as the commander-in-chief of the forces of the empire, or as an independent prince.

The Rajah of Colapore is of the same family as the Rajah of Suttarah; he is consequently addressed by the Peishwah as his superior, and treated by him as such on all occasions of public ceremony. His territories extend along the sea coast of the Conkan, immediately to the N. of the Portuguese territory of Goa. He usually maintains fifteen hundred horse, and three thousand peons, and his territories are said to yield a revenue of about thirty lacks of rupees.

Mulhar Row Holkar, the founder of this family, was a person of obscure birth, but of distinguished courage. He escaped, as we have seen, from the battle of Paniput, and died in 1766, at Mulhar Ghur, a small fortress in one of his Jagheers, about forty miles from Calpee.

Janajee Scindiah was born at Pullalee, near Poonah; he rose in the service of Bajeerow the first Peishwah, and accompanied him in an expedition that was undertaken towards the close of Sahoojee's reign, against the province of Malwa, which was divided between the Rajah of Suttarah, the Peishwah, and Mulhar Row Holkar. As a reward for the services which Scindiah rendered in this expedition, he received a considerable portion of the Peishwah and

Timour, exasperated against each other, did not observe, until too late, that their quarrels had nursed a new enemy, which threatened the extinction of every Mahomedan government in India; the Mahrattas fattened on the spoils of the Mogul empire, which, torn by civil dissensions, could offer no opposition to their encroachments; and there cannot be a doubt, that they would have succeeded in establishing their dominion over the whole of the Peninsula, had it not been for the misconduct of the Bhow previous to the battle of Paniput, and the growing influence of England. It is an empire which has risen on the basis of injustice, falsehood, and treachery; force, intrigue, and evasion, have

---

Rajah of Suttarah's share, which grant was afterwards confirmed in jagheer to his descendants by the Rajah of Suttarah. Janajee was succeeded by his fifth son Madajee, who by degrees contrived to get possession of the remaining forts of Malwa, which belonged to the Poonah state.

The family of Guickwar is one of the most ancient in the Mahratta country; they have long been in possession of the greater part of Guzzerat.

The Putwurden, Purtaneddee, and Rastiah families, also, possess great influence in the southern Mahratta country.—Vide *Notes on the Mahratta War.*

alternately been employed to pave the way to greatness; and the craft and subtlety of a Mahratta has passed into a proverb. No power ever placed confidence in them, without ultimately having reason to repent of its credulity; their motives are ever selfish, and the sacrifice of the means to the end, may be regarded as an invariable maxim of their state policy. The same ideas, and the same principles, are alike familiar to the Peishwah, and the meanest cooly in his camp; plunder has always been their avowed object, and hence it was, that their armies consisted only of large undisciplined bodies of irregular horse, until experience taught them that, without the aid of infantry and artillery, their attempts to take possession of places of strength would generally terminate in discomfiture. This led to the introduction of European officers, and to the formation of regular battalions, and this it was which, by inducing them to risk a general engagement, with better disciplined troops, occasioned their defeats at Paniput and during the late Mahratta war.

The chieftains of the Mahratta confederacy have never been united by any constitutional law, and although they acknowledge the Rajah of Suttarah as the hereditary head of the empire, and yield a nominal, indefinite, obedience to the Peishwah, as the first executive officer of the state, they are, in every sense of the term, independent, and admit of no interference in the internal administration of their affairs. Princes, who possess the power of following their own inclinations, seldom suffer themselves to be bound by civil institutions or established laws; and therefore, like the potentates of Germany the leading chiefs of the Mahrattas have not hesitated to make war upon each other, and even upon the head of the empire. We have witnessed, in our own times, the claim of the Rajah of Berar to the situation of Peishwah; the efforts of Dowlut Row Scindiah to usurp the supreme authority, and the overthrow of the latter by Jeswunt Row Holkar, under the walls of the Peishwah's palace. As the constitutional representative of the Sovereigns, the power of the Peishwah to conclude all general treaties connected with the states, was formerly acknowledged by the chiefs; but they now assert, and have exercised, a right to form treaties and alliances without his advice or concurrence*.

The Mahratta princes have no regular system of jurisprudence for the internal administration of affairs in their respective dominions. Justice is unknown, and flattery, perfidy, and cunning, are the only means of ensuring safety or advancement. If the person at the head of the government be bold and enterprising, he will become a despot, and at the head of an army enforce implicit obedience to his orders. But if his spirit be feeble, and his disposition indolent, he will soon lose all his authority, his court will become the centre of intrigue and corruption, he will be unable to collect his revenues, and the oppressions of corrupt ministers will drive the villagers into exile, or provoke open insurrection. A more distinct notion, however, of the internal management of a Mahratta province, will be

---

* All the treaties made by the English with the Mahrattas previous to the war of 1803, were concluded with the Peishwah; his territories being less remote than those of any of the other chiefs, our interests were more immediately connected with his, and the situation of Peishwah had not then sunk into its present insignificance.

given by subjoining a short account of the jagheedar system, as it has existed since the conquests of Bajeerow.

The Mahratta soldiers receive no regular pay, but it was customary to grant to their commanders, the revenue of certain districts for the subsistence of their troops *. These lands were consequently held on a military tenure, and subject to resumption at the will of the sovereign; but they have almost invariably become hereditary, either from a want of inclination, or of ability, in the government to resume them. The larger portion of the Mahratta country is divided into jagheers of this nature; their possessors collect the rents from the ryots at their own discretion, and pay their kists †, or yield obedience to the sovereign in exact proportion to his power of coercion. Those petty chiefs frequently make war upon each other, and he who is more able or enterprising than his neighbour, gradually rises into power

* The revenues of a district are frequently assigned for a stated period to such persons as may have incurred any extraordinary expense on account of the circar, or have otherwise become its creditors.—*See India Reports.*

† Kist signifies instalment.

and consequence, as may be exemplified in a thousand instances. They pay a peishcush, or tribute, to the sovereign, who has no right to demand more than the sum originally agreed upon, and who never interferes in the internal management of the jagheer, or in the cultivation of the lands. In the event of war, all these chiefs are commanded to assemble their quotas of troops, who are permitted to share indiscriminately in all the plunder they can procure: and since in a government thus constituted, every thing must depend on the vigour and efficiency of the executive authority, a weak prince, unsupported by foreign aid, would either be deposed or sink into insignificance; while, on the other hand, a man of genius, of active pursuits, will always endeavour to encroach upon the liberties of his subjects, and the rights of his neighbours.

CHAP. II.

BALLAJEE ROW, the late Peishwah, who, as I have already observed, did not live to witness the consequences of a battle, which had broken the power and splendour of his country, left two sons, Mada Row and Narrain Row, neither of whom had attained to years of maturity at the time of his death, (1761). Mada Row was declared successor to the situation of Peishwah, but the factious cabals of his uncle, Ragonath Row, (or as he was usually called, Ragobah), who wished to possess himself of the supreme authority, disturbed the early part of his reign, and involved the Poonah state in a war with Nizam Ali Khan, the new soubahdar of the Deckan *. Ragobah, who appears to have been a person of a weak mind, but a turbulent and ambitious disposition, disappointed

* MSS.

in his hopes, and apprehensive of his personal safety, fled from Poonah, and threw himself upon the protection of the Nizam; who, readily availing himself of so favourable an opportunity to recover the territories so lately wrested from his brother, despatched Morad Khan with an army to support the claims of Ragobah. This general succeeded in surprising the camp of the Mahrattas, by swimming the river Beemah * in the night, at the head of a chosen body of horse; and had the singular good fortune to seize and carry off the person of the Peishwah from the midst of his army †. The surrender of Dowlutabad, with countries yielding a revenue of nine lacks of rupees, was the stipulated price of his liberty ‡; but an alliance purchased on such terms could not be of lasting duration, hostilities were renewed,

* The river Beemah rises in the mountains to the N. E. of Poonah; and after bathing the walls of Punderpoor, enters the Kistna, near the town of Firozeghur. This is one of the most beautiful rivers in the Mahratta territory, and is deemed sacred by the Hindoos. It contains a large volume of water during the rains, and is passed on boats at Punderpoor.

† MSS. ‡ MSS.

and while the Mahrattas cruelly ravaged the districts around Hyderabad *, the Nizam advanced upon Poonah, which was once more abandoned to the flames †. Ragonath Row, who had been reconciled to his nephew, revenged the destruction of Poonah by a victory over the Mahomedan army, on the banks of the Godaverry ‡, which eventually led to a peace, concluded towards the close of 1763 §. In this war neither Holkar nor Scindiah took any part; and Janajee Bhonslah, Rajah of Berar, openly sided with the Nizam ||.

* Hyderabad is the capital of the Nizam's dominions, situated on the banks of the Moosa river, in latitude 17° 15' N., longitude, 78° 42' E. It was founded in the year 1585; it is a place of no strength, but is surrounded by a wall seven or eight miles in circumference; it has a fine appearance when viewed from a distance, but its streets are narrow and filthy.

† It was never the policy of the Mahrattas to defend their capital, or indeed any of their cities. Their wives and treasures were usually placed in strong hill forts, while they kept the field with their armies.

‡ One of the finest rivers in the Deckan, has its source in the western Ghauts between Poonah and Surat; it crosses nearly the whole of the peninsula from W. to E., and after dividing itself in the district of Rajahmundry, enters the bay of Bengal by several different mouths.

§ MSS. || MSS.

The civil dissensions at Poonah, together with the war between the Nizam and the Peishwah, had induced Hyder Ali, the Mysorean general, to invade the Mahratta territories; and his efforts were at first attended with such success, that Mada Row took the field in person, and crossed the Kistna in March, 1764. The army of the Peishwah was somewhat superior in numbers to that of his enemy *, but the latter was better disciplined and equipped, and occupied a strong position near Savanore †.

---

* The force under Hyder Ali amounted to about sixty thousand men, divided into nearly equal portions of cavalry, infantry, and irregular peons, armed with matchlocks, and supported by twenty pieces of cannon. The Mahrattas are said to have consisted of forty thousand foot, with a small train of unwieldy and ill-served guns.—*Wilkes.*

† Shahnoor or Savanore is an ancient town in the kingdom of Beejepoor, situated in latitude 15° 1′ N., longitude, 75° 22′ E. It is a capital of a province of the same name, and was long the residence of a Pattan family which governed the country between the Toombudra and the Kistna. The town is small and surrounded with a wall, but is a place of no strength, and now in a state of decay. The principality of Savanore, when attacked by the Peishwah and Salabat Jung in 1756, consisted of twenty-two districts, and now includes the greater part of the territory belonging to the Mahrattas, south of the Kistna.

Mujeed Khan, the grandfather of the present nabob,

Madar Row displayed considerable military talent in this campaign; and his genius, from the commencement to the termination of the war, prevailed over that of Hyder, who, discomfited in all his plans, and beaten in every action, was forced to sue for peace. A treaty was accordingly concluded * in the

---

unable to withstand the combined attack of the Peishwah and the Nizam, was compelled to purchase a peace by the surrender of half of his possessions to his enemies. This prince was succeeded by his son Hakeem Khan, who, having contracted an intimate alliance with Hyder Ali, recovered, with the assistance of that chief, the districts of which his father had been deprived, and passed the remainder of his life in prosperity; but his death, which occurred in 1782, was followed by the ruin of his family, who were attacked and driven into exile by Tippoo. When peace was concluded in 1792, Savanore fell to the share of the Peishwah, who granted that town and the adjoining districts to Hussein Khan, the second son of Hakeem Khan; but Kheir Khan, the elder brother, having obtained from Nana Furnavese a decision in his favour, was put in possession of his patrimony by Purseram Bhow, who had received instructions from Poonah to that effect. The Khan has ever since continued to reside at Savanore, but his country has continued in so distracted a state, that he has never been able to collect the revenues.

* Ragobah, who acted as mediator, is accused of having betrayed the interests of his nephew. Hyder's usurpation of Sera was tacitly admitted, and all discussions relative to

month of October, by Hyder, who engaged to restore the territories he had taken from Moraris Row, of Gootie, to relinquish his claims on the province of Savanore, and to pay thirty-two lacks of rupees *.

The Peishwah retired with his army towards the north, about the end of February, 1765, and employed himself in regulating the internal affairs of his territories, and improving his capital. In the following year he again took the field against the Rajah of Berar, who was the hereditary enemy of his family, and who had long endeavoured to procure for himself the situation of Peishwah, which he claimed as his birthright. The alliance, or rather the neutrality of Nizam Ali Khan, was, on this occasion, solicited by both parties; and as it was the design of that prince to promote the disputes of the Mahratta chiefs, he declared in favour of the Peishwah, with whom he had a personal conference on the banks of the Poornah †. In this war the confederates were

---

the Polygars of Chittledroog, Riadroog, and Harpanooly, were studiously and intentionally avoided.—For an excellent account of this war, see *Wilkes's South of India*.

* See Wilkes.

† The dominions of the Nizam and those of the Rajah

successful*; the Rajah sued for peace, and Mada Row returned to Poonah, in order to suppress the dangerous intrigues of his uncle, whom he had imprudently made his Dewan †. The latter years of his life were clouded by domestic quarrels, which were pushed to such a length, that Ragonath was thrown into prison, whence he did not obtain his release until a short time previous to the death of the Peishwah which occurred in 1772 ‡.

Mada Row was succeeded by Narrain Row, the second son of Ballajee Row, a person who does not seem to have inherited any share of the ability or courage of his brother. He fell a sacrifice to family feuds soon after his accession to the musnud, and was assassinated at the instigation of his uncle, who openly avowed his intention of seizing the

---

of Berar, were adjoining to, and even intermixed with each other, in such a manner that no proper line of demarcation could be drawn. Their subjects were consequently engaged in continual disputes, and it had long been the wish of the Nizam to recover the western parts of Berar, of which his predecessors had been deprived by the Bhonslah family.

* MSS.

† MSS.

‡ Notes on the late Mahratta war.

reins of government*. But in this he was opposed by the nobles of the court, and the chieftains of the empire, who held the crime of assassination in abhorrence†; he was driven from Poonah, and the posthumous son of Narrain Row was proclaimed Peishwah, by the influence of twelve chiefs, under the name of Bara Chye, or the twelve brothers‡. The principal actor in these transactions was Ballajee Pundit, who caused himself to be declared Regent; and who, under the name of Nana Furnavese, governed the Poonah state with distinguished ability for upwards of twenty years.

A civil war now ensued, in which the confederates were assisted by Nizam Ali Khan and the Rajah of Berar. Ragobah was entirely defeated in the plains of Arass, in the province of Guzzerat, and was indebted for his personal safety to the fleetness of his horse§. He embarked in an open

* India Papers.

† The murder of a Bramin is, in the eyes of the Hindoos, a crime of the first magnitude, and the punishment of death is never awarded under the Hindoo law, to people of that caste.

‡ MSS.

§ MSS.

boat at a port in the Gulf of Cambay; and, with the view of demanding succour from the English, landed at Surat, in 1775. But before I proceed to give an account of the series of events resulting from this occurrence, it may be well to take a short view of the then existing connexion between the British Government and the court of Poonah.

The contiguity of Bombay to Baglama and the Conkan, the original possessions of the Mahrattas, rendered it the interest of the East India Company to maintain a friendly intercourse with the Rajah of Suttarah, and in 1674, Sevajee had granted them his permission to trade in any part of his dominions: but the conquest of Salsette and Bassein *, in 1739, awakened the fears of the Bombay council, and thenceforward it was thought necessary to get possession of the above places †.

The flight of Ragobah presented a fair

* It is situated in lat. 19° 18′ N., and only separated from Salsette by a narrow strait. It formerly belonged to the Portuguese, who had obtained it, in 1531, from the Rajah of Cambay, by whom it was fortified.—*Hamilton.*

† Asiatic Annual Register for 1804.

occasion for the accomplishment of their wishes, and the government of Bombay incautiously promised to place him at the head of an empire, from which he had so lately been ignominiously driven, upon condition that he should cede to the Company, in perpetual sovereignty, the islands of Salsette and Caranja, together with the port of Bassein*. These terms were agreed to by the exiled prince, and the places in question were soon afterwards taken possession of by the British troops. A small force was sent into Guzzerat, which after having reduced the fortress of Baroach †, joined the cavalry of their ally, and advanced into the interior. Scindiah and the Bhonslah appeared in the field to defend the rights of the infant Peishwah, but they were defeated in turn ‡, and Ragobah would have entered Poonah in triumph, had not an unforeseen circumstance blighted all his hopes. The Supreme

* India Reports.

† Is the capital of a district of the same name in Guzzerat, situated on the north bank of the Nerbudda, about twenty-five miles above its junction with the sea.—Lat. 21° 41′ N.; long. 73° 60′ E.

‡ India Papers.

Government entirely disapproved of the measures of the Bombay council, the British troops were recalled, and Colonel Upton was deputed to negotiate a peace with the Mahratta states *.

This officer, in conformity with his instructions, proceeded to Poonah; and a treaty, confirming the cession of Salsette, and giving a grant of Baroach to the Company †, was signed at Poorunder on the 1st of March 1776 ‡. The stipulations of this treaty were never carried fully into effect, the pacific views of the Governor-General were counteracted by the intrigues of France, and another rupture soon afterwards ensued. But before I proceed to relate the principal events of a war which lasted for several years, and brought the Company's affairs to the brink of ruin, it will be necessary to offer a few observations on the state of parties at Poonah.

---

* India Papers.

† The ministers of the Peishwah were at the same time obliged to surrender the districts of Cundlapoor, Jaulnah, and the fortress of Dowletabad, to the Nizam, as an equivalent for the services he had rendered them during the war.

‡ India Papers.

The factious spirit which had so long distracted the Mahratta empire, still raged with unabated violence, and the unstable nature of the government, with an infant at its head, opened a wide field of ambition to the military chiefs, which form that heterogeneous confederacy. Each was bent on individual plans of advancement, and only anxious to build his own fortune on the ruin of his rivals. Ragobah asserted his claims to the office of Peishwah, by maintaining the illegitimacy of Narrain Row, and his own right under the Hindoo law to an equal share of the family possessions*. Madajee Scindiah had acquired great power and reputation by his conquests in Hindostan, and expected, through the means of Nana Furnavese, to usurp the supreme authority; while the Bhonslah looked upon the family of Bajeerow as the invaders of his rights, and claimed the supremacy as the

* It is a custom among the Mahrattas, that when any chief dies, his son, though an infant, shall succeed to the employments he may have held under government, while a division of the property is made among the family and relations of the deceased.

nearest relation of the Rajah of Suttarah *. Purseram Bhow and Hurry Punt †, (names familiar to the English) were engaged in war with Hyder Ali Khan ‡, and Nana Furnavese, who, with the assistance of Scindiah and Holkar, had succeeded in establishing his authority at Poonah, kept the infant Peishwah, together with his mother, shut up in the fortress of Poorunder. He detested the English as the supporters of Ragobah, and turned his thoughts towards the French, to whom he offered an establishment on the coast of the Conkan. This gave rise to his connexion with the Chevalier St. Luben, whose arrival excited the most extravagant apprehensions in the council at Bombay, and hurried them into measures which proved injurious to their employers.

---

* MSS. and India Papers.

† They both held large jagheers in the southern frontier.

‡ Hurry Punt was deserted by a great part of his army, who went over to Hyder. Holkar and Scindiah were requested to march to his assistance, but refused to obey. The Nizam was then solicited to come forward, but he would do nothing unless he was put in possession of Ahmednuggur. These occurrences took place in the beginning of 1778.

After a variety of negotiations, in which the pusillanimous conduct of the one, was opposed by the falsehood and subterfuge of the other, the Governor-General was induced to espouse the cause of Ragobah, as the only means of destroying the growing influence of France. Nothing could, however, be more ill-timed than the line of policy pursued by the British Government on this occasion; our troops had been withdrawn in the plenitude of success, when our ally had a strong party in his favour, and a victorious army at his back *. But a melancholy change had since taken place in the situation of his affairs; his friends disgusted at our fluctuating proceedings, had abandoned his cause, and his army had either dispersed or entered the service of his rivals. Mr. Hastings was nevertheless resolved, by the bold and decisive measure of march-

* The leaders of this party were Tukojee Holkar, the successor of Mulhar Row, Marha Furnavese, Bukaba Pundit, and Succaram Bapoo, the rival of Nana, and the person who had negotiated the treaty of Poorunder. They invited Ragobah to assume the regency, but he imagining that they were actuated by selfish motives, placed little reliance on their promises.

ing an army across the peninsula, from Bengal to Baglama *, to carry the war into the centre of the enemy's country. Overtures were made to the Rajah of Berar through Mr. Elliot, who was deputed, with the view of detaching him from the confederacy, and who was empowered to offer him the full support of the Governor-General in his claims to the possessions of the Rajah of Suttarah, and to the situation of Peishwah. Mr. Hastings at the same time professed a desire to secure the friendship of the Nizam; but that prince openly avowed his enmity to Ragobah, and declared his resolution to oppose his return to Poonah. A defensive alliance was formed with the Rana of Gohud, whose provinces lay open to the invasion of Scindiah, and who looked for protection to the British government †.

The Council of Bombay had, in conformity with their instructions, concluded a new treaty with the exiled prince, and assembled a force at Ballapoor ‡, consisting

---

* India Records.

† India Records.

‡ A small fort on the continent, at the head of Bombay harbour.

of five hundred and fifty Europeans, and about three thousand Sepoys, commanded by Colonel Egerton, who was accompanied by two civil commissioners, vested with powers nearly equal to those of the commander, a species of divided authority, which must ever prove fatal to the operations of the army in which it exists. Colonel Egerton, instead of advancing rapidly upon Poonah, which he might have surprised, pitched his camp at Campooly, at the foot of the Bhore Ghaut *, where he patiently awaited the tardy motions of Ragobah, whose dilatoriness could only be attributed to his anticipation of the result. The army, at last put in motion, was harassed by the Mahratta horse, which had ample time to collect, and was led by Scindiah, the most skilful of the Mahratta generals. On the 10th of January, 1779, they beheld from the heights, which overlook the Mahratta capital, that city reduced to ashes; the adjacent country laid waste, and bodies of horse hovering round in every direction. Colonel Egerton had some time before, either

* The principal pass on the great road from Bombay to Poonah, situate about thirty miles from the latter.

from ill health or disgust, resigned the command; and that trust was now reposed in Colonel Cockburn, who held a council of war at which it was resolved to retreat; and although even Ragobah remonstrated in the strongest manner against so disgraceful a proceeding, the army retired to Worgaum, where they took up a position. Here a council of war was once more convened; and strange and incomprehensible as it may seem, the commander declared that his troops were unable to force a passage, and entirely at the mercy of the enemy *.

A deputation was accordingly sent to Scindiah, charged with a communication to the following effect, That the expedition had been undertaken from an erroneous conception, that the principal Mahratta chiefs were in favour of Ragobah's elevation to the Regency; but, being now convinced that their information was defective, they desired a cessation of hostilities, and permission for the army to

* That a British officer, at the head of five hundred Europeans and five thousand Sepoys, with a good train of artillery, should publicly pronounce such a force unable to make good its retreat for about fifty miles, through a body of predatory horse, must ever appear incredible, and can only be attributed to infatuation.

retire unmolested. Scindiah insisted that Ragobah should be unconditionally delivered up to him, and that all the acquisitions of the Company, since 1756, should be restored to the Peishwah, with the exception of Baroach, which was to be ceded to himself. These disgraceful terms were accepted, Ragobah was delivered into the hands of his most inveterate foe, two English gentlemen were given up as hostages for the fulfilment of the treaty, and the army was permitted to return in safety to Bombay*.

In the spring of 1778, the army, designed to be sent from Bengal to the western coast, was ordered to rendezvous at Calpee†; it consisted of six battalions of Sepoys, and a proportionate train of artillery, commanded by Colonel Leslie, an old and experienced officer. Holkar and Scindiah offered the detachment a passage through their territories to Guzzerat, but another route was preferred, since little dependence could be

---

* Colonel Cockburn was afterwards cashiered, by orders from home.—Consult India Papers for an account of this campaign.

† Calpee, a town in the province of Agra, on the S.W. side of the Jumna.

placed on the promises of these chieftains, whose sentiments were known to be at variance with their professions. The force was assembled in April, and Colonel Leslie was empowered to negotiate with the different chiefs, through whose countries he might pass, and particularly instructed to renew those negotiations with the Rajah of Berar, which the unexpected death of Mr. Elliot had suspended*. The promises of that chief were fair, but his conduct was evasive and Mahratta-like; he seemed desirous of waiting the result of the campaign, before he entered into any arrangement. Colonel Goddard, who had succeeded Colonel Leslie in the command†, kept to the north of Berar, and continued his march through Bundelcund and Bhopaul to the Nerbudda, which he crossed at Hoosingabad‡. The army had encountered

* India Papers.

† Colonel Leslie had incurred the displeasure of the Supreme Government by his great delay, and orders were issued to remove him from the command, but before these orders were received he had retired.

‡ Hoosingabad, or rather Hussainabad, is a strong fort on the S. bank of the Nerbudda, in lat. 22° 40′ N.; long. 77° 53′ E. It formerly belonged to the Nabob of Bhopaul, from whom it was taken by the Rajah of Berar, and may be termed the key of the Deckan from Hindostan.

little or no opposition*; it was abundantly supplied with provisions in Bundelcund, and received the most friendly assistance from the Nabob of Bhopaul. From Hoosingabad Colonel Goddard advanced to Boorhanpoor†, the ancient capital of Candeish, and in conformity with the wishes of the Bombay government, directed his march to the banks of the Tapti, where he arrived in February, 1779. He was nominated, some time after his arrival, to the chief command of the Bombay army‡, and by a series of skilful operations, retrieved the honour of the British arms, and effaced the stain which they had received at Worgaum. He opened the campaign on the 1st of January, 1780, by passing the Tapti, and on the 17th he invested Dhubay§, which immediately fell into his hands. Futty Sing

---

* Ballajee Pundit, the Peishwah's general, made a slight effort to oppose the passage of the Cani, but he was quickly put to flight.

† This was once a large and magnificent city, but is now in ruins. It is situated on the N. bank of the Tapti, two hundred and ninety-six miles from Poonah, and one hundred and fifty from Oujein.

‡ India Papers.

§ This city is said to be very ancient, and is situated about forty miles N. E. of Baroach.—*Hamilton*.

Guickwar, the Mahratta chief of Guzzerat, alarmed at the progress of the British army, concluded a treaty with its commander; by which it was stipulated, that they should protect each other from all foreign enemies, and exclude the government of Poonah from any share of territory in the province of Guzzerat; that the province should for the future be equally divided between Futty Sing and the Honourable Company; that Ahmedabad and its dependencies should be allotted to the Guickwar; that the British Government should support their new ally, in withholding the tribute paid by him to the Peishwah, and that he should make over to them his district S. of the Tapti, as well as that of Zinnore, and some villages in the Pergunnah of Baroach. General Goddard then laid siege to Ahmedabad, which surrendered in a few days, although garrisoned with eight thousand Arabs. Scindiah and Holkar were advancing upon Surat with the design of surprising that city, but on the British army moving to meet them, Scindiah professed an anxiety for peace, and proposed that Ragobah (who had effected his escape) should retire on a pension, that his infant son Bajeerow should be made Dewan, and that he, Scindiah, should discharge the duties of the office until Bajeerow became of age. These arrangements being evidently calculated to throw the whole power of the Mahratta empire into Scindiah's hands, were deemed inadmissible; and, on the 22d of March, General Goddard made a movement in the hopes of being able to attack the enemy, whose camp he surprised on the night of the 3d of April, putting the whole of his troops to flight. The approach of the monsoon put a stop to further active operation; General Goddard returned to Broderah, and the campaign terminated with a brilliant action fought by Major Forbes near Zinnore, and with the defeat of a large body of Mahrattas, by a small corps under Lieutenant Welsh, in which the former lost the whole of their artillery and baggage*.

During these occurrences in Guzzerat, an equal degree of success attended our arms in Gohud, where Captain Popham defeated the enemy in several battles; but the detachment under his command was quite inadequate to the services required of it, and Sir

* India Papers and Reports.

Eyre Coote, in a letter which he addressed to Mr. Hastings, represented in the most forcible manner the great injury to be apprehended from the employment of inefficient means, and the policy of never undertaking any expedition without an almost absolute certainty of success, in order, that the impression, entertained by the natives of our great superiority in arms, might not be removed*. Captain Popham, notwithstanding the smallness of his detachment, succeeded in all his operations, and finished the campaign by the capture of Gwalior, a fortress hitherto deemed impregnable by the natives of Hindostan†, and garrisoned with a thousand men.

The Bombay government having determined upon the siege of Bassein, the army was ordered to march from Guzzerat, and arrived before that place on the 13th of

* India Papers.

† This fortress is situated on the summit of a lofty rock, perpendicular on all sides, excepting that by which the assailants carried it. Even there, the scarp at the top was sixteen feet in height, and the wall thirty feet. The party advanced silently in the night, and escaladed the wall, whilst the garrison, confiding in the strength of the place, were locked in sleep.

November. General Goddard conducted the operations of the siege with regularity and precaution, and on the 11th of December the town surrendered at discretion *. The General then put himself at the head of his troops, and having forced the Ghauts took up a position on their summits, where he spent some months in attempting to bring about an accommodation; but Nana Furnavese, elated with the success of Hyder in the Carnatic, not only rejected every proposal, but sent a body of horse into the Conkan to intercept the retreat of our army. It being adviseable that the troops should retire before the commencement of the rains, the retreat was begun in the mouth of April; and after having defeated and dispersed the Mahrattas † amounting to upwards of forty thousand men, the army was placed in cantonments, and no other movement of consequence was

* Upwards of two hundred pieces of cannon, and a considerable quantity of ammunition was found in the place.—*India Papers*.

† The Mahratta army, which consisted of forty thousand horse, about six thousand bad infantry, and several pieces of artillery, endeavoured to intercept General Goddard between the villages of Chawkey and Burwab, but were repulsed with severe loss.

made on the W. coast of India, during the year 1781*.

Colonel Camac, who had been appointed to the command of a detachment to act on the W. of the Jumna, drove the enemy from Gohud, and advanced as far as Seronje† in Malwa; but disappointed of the aid promised him by the Nabob of Bhopaul, and greatly straitened for provisions‡, he deemed it necessary to fall back towards Calpee. He broke up from Seronje on the 7th of March, and on the third day he reached Mahautpoor, harassed by the Mahratta cavalry under the command of Scindiah in person. Here he took up a position with the view of provoking the enemy to a battle, and on the 24th surprised and routed him, taking ten pieces of cannon§, and nearly the whole of his ammunition and baggage. The detachment then continued its retreat, and was soon afterwards joined by Colonel

* India Papers.

† Seronje is a large town, situated in an open and fertile country, one hundred and seventy miles N. E. of Oujein and two hundred and fifty from Agra. It now belongs to Ameer Khan.

‡ The country had been entirely laid waste by Scindiah.

§ India Papers.

Muir, with three battalions of infantry and two of cavalry. Colonel Muir, being the senior officer, assumed the command, and his instructions were, to advance to Oujein, Scindiah's capital, in order to negotiate a peace, provided the Mahrattas felt equally disposed for a termination of hostilities.

To take a cursory view of the situation of affairs at this period, towards the end of 1779, Hyder Ali Khan, who had defeated the Mahrattas in many battles, and made himself master of Chittledroog and several districts, as far N. as the Kistna, formed an alliance with the Nizam, the Peishwah, and Ragojee Bhonslah, by which it was stipulated that their united arms should be turned against the English. That the Peishwah and Scindiah should prosecute the war on the western coast, Hyder Ali invade the Carnatic, the Nizam march an army into the northern circars, and the Rajah of Berar attack the province of Orissa. But this coalition was attended with the same results as most other confederacies, where mutual jealousies prevail, and where the contracting parties recognise no motives but selfish interests. Scindiah's motions were languid; the Nizam promised much, but did nothing; the Rajah of Berar was evidently forced to become a member of the coalition against his inclination; and Hyder Ali alone fulfilled his part of the agreement, by overrunning the Carnatic with a powerful army. He advanced almost to the gates of Madras, and in a pitched battle, fought near Truoallum, on the 10th of September, 1780*, defeated the English army, under Colonel Baillie, with great slaughter. The extremities to which the government of Fort St. George was reduced by this memorable defeat, in which they had lost the flower of their army, rendered it necessary that immediate succour should be furnished from Bengal†. Sir Eyre Coote was accordingly despatched by sea, with a strong detachment of Europeans, and it was resolved that a force of five thousand Sepoys should follow as soon as possible, by Cuttack‡. The conduct of the Rajah of

---

* Memoirs of the War in Asia.

† India Papers.

‡ In conformity with the tenor of the coalition, the Bhonslah had assembled at Nagpoor, in the autumn of 1779, a body of thirty thousand horse, intended, as was given out, to invade Bahar, under the command of his son. They took

Berar had shewn that he harboured no hostile intentions towards us, and as it was desirable that an open rupture should be avoided, Mr. Anderson* was deputed to his son Chimnajee Bapoo, who commanded an army in Cuttack, to explain the wishes of the Supreme Government, as well as their determination to force a passage for the detachment, in the event of its being refused. Mr. Anderson had several interviews with the Prince, who at last agreed to conclude, on the part of his father, an offensive and defensive alliance with the Company, which was afterwards ratified by the Governor-General and the Bhonslah. By this treaty, which broke the coalition, it was stipulated that the Company should pay the Rajah thirteen lacks of rupees, and assist him in

---

a different route however, and, by studied delay, did not reach Cuttack until the end of May, 1780, when the periodical rains put a stop to all military operations.

* Previous to this, however, the draft of a treaty with the Poonah government had been sent to Nagpoor, and the Rajah had been requested to act as mediator and guarantee. His reply was received in July, 1781; but it contained so many objections to the proposed draft, that there was no hope of an immediate accommodation with the Peishwab.

the conquest of Ghurra * Mandela, and the cities of Boorhanpoor and Asseerghur†, which had been lately ceded by the Peishwah to Scindiah. The Rajah of Berar, in return, agreed to furnish the detachment under Colonel Pierce with two thousand horse, in the war against Hyder. One of the most powerful states was thus detached from the confederacy, the beneficial effects of which were soon felt, and it hastened a peace with Scindiah, which was concluded by Colonel Muir, on the 13th of October, 1781.

By this treaty it was agreed, that Scindiah should endeavour to effect an accommodation between the Belligerents, that the country on the right bank of the Jumna, taken by the English, should be restored to Scindiah, and that he should not molest the territories of the Rana of Gohud, or any of the chiefs in alliance with the Company‡. It is worthy of remark, that in concluding this

---

* A district in the province of Candeish.

† The strongest fortress in Candeish, taken by Colonel Stephenson in the late Mahratta war, and now belonging to Scindiah.

‡ It was also stipulated, that Scindiah should restore the possessions of Rajah Ramchunder, and place him on the musnud in the presence of Colonel Muir.

treaty, Scindiah acted as an independent Prince, and seemed perfectly indifferent as to what the Peishwah, or his other allies, might think of his conduct.

The court of Poonah, thus deprived of the support of the two most powerful chiefs of the empire, and jealous at the same time of the conquest of Hyder Ali, expressed a desire for peace, which after the lapse of several months spent in negotiations, was at last concluded through the mediation of Scindiah*. By this treaty, which consisted of seventeen articles, it was stipulated—That all countries, cities, and fortresses, which have been taken from the Peishwah since the peace of Poorunder † should be restored to him, that the islands of Salsette, Elephanta, Caranja ‡, and Hog, should continue in possession of the Company: that the Mahratta chiefs should cede to the Company all right and title to the city of Baroach, relinquishing the choute, and every other claim whatsoever: that the English should abandon, in

* India Papers.

† A strong fortress, seventeen miles S. E from Poonah.

‡ A small and beautiful island in the harbour of Bombay.

favour of the Peishwah, a tract of territory yielding three lacks of rupees, and ceded to the Company by Colonel Upton's treaty: that Ragonath Row should be allowed four months from the conclusion of the treaty to fix on a place of residence; and that, after that period, the Company should neither afford him support nor protection; the Peishwah, on his part, agreeing not to molest him, and to grant a pension of twenty thousand rupees per month for his support: that the allies of both states should be invited to become parties in the treaty: that the territory possessed by the Guickwar, at the commencement of the war, should still remain in his possession, but that he should, for the future, pay the customary tribute to the Peishwah, and perform such services as had heretofore been established. That Hyder Ali Khan should be made to relinquish all such territories belonging to the English and their allies, as he had taken possession of since his treaty with the Peishwah, and that the same territories should be delivered over to the Company, or Mahomed Ali Khan, within the space of six months from the ratification of the treaty. The contracting parties mutually agreed that the vessels of each should have free access to the ports of the other; that their subjects should enjoy, without interruption, the privileges of trade; and that the Peishwah should not suffer any new European settlements in his own territories, or in those of his dependant chiefs, nor the English afford assistance to any power at enmity with the Peishwah. The above are the principal articles of this treaty, which was guaranteed by Scindiah, and signed at Salbhye on the 17th of May, 1782; by Scindiah on the part of the Mahrattas, and Mr. David Anderson on that of the Company*.

* Indian Treaties

CHAP. III.

BY the conclusion of this peace, the Company were relieved from the danger and expense of a ruinous war, and the Mahrattas, left unshackled, had leisure to prosecute their conquests in Hindostan *. The assassination of Afrasiab Khan, in 1784, and the distractions which then prevailed at Delhi, put the person of the unfortunate Shah Allum into the possession of Scindiah, who, in the name of the Peishwah, assumed the title of Vakeel ool Mootluck, or, Chief Commissioner. The degraded representative of Timour was nominally allowed sixty thousand rupees per mensem, for the expense of his household, but he could only be regarded as a state prisoner accompany-

* Soon after the peace of Salbhye, the Peishwah became involved in an unsuccessful struggle with the new Sultan of Mysore, who made himself master of the strong fort of Darwar, and many districts in the southern frontier.

ing the Mahratta camp, to sanction the conquests and depredations of Scindiah, who in this manner made himself master of Agra and Alighur*. In 1787 he failed in an attempt to collect the choute from the Rajahs of Jyepoor and Joudipoor, and driven with precipitation across the Chumbul †, was constrained to evacuate the provinces of Delhi and Agra; but he soon recovered from the effects of this disaster, and returning to the charge, expelled the Rohillas from Delhi, and put their leader, the infamous Gholam Khadir, to an ignominious death ‡.

* Scott.

† This river has its source near the ancient city of Mundu, in the centre of the province of Malwa, within fifteen miles of the Nerbudda. From thence it pursues a north-easterly direction; and, after washing the city of Kotah, and receiving many smaller streams, it falls into the Jumna, twenty miles below Etaweh. The breadth of its channel at the ford Kyteree, near Dhool-poor, is three quarters of a mile, and the whole length of its course four hundred and forty miles. At Keyteree, the southern bank is bold and lofty; and, in the rainy season, when the channel is full, the prospect of such a body of water, bounded by hills of various shapes, forms a contrast to the vast plains between the Jumna and the Ganges.—*Hamilton*.

‡ This wretch had contrived, after the defeat of Scin-

Henceforward Scindiah became the most powerful prince in Hindostan: his sway extended over the most fertile provinces of the Mogul empire, and his power was felt from the Tapti to the Ganges. He was indebted for many of these conquests to M. de Boigue*, a Savoyard, who had entered his service soon after the treaty of Salbhye, and

---

diah, to get the person of the unfortunate Shah into his hands. He dethroned him, deprived him of sight, and treated him, as well as the other members of the imperial family, with the most wanton barbarity.—*Scott.*

* M. de Boigue was a native of Savoy, and served first in the French, and afterwards in the Russian service, during which period he became acquainted with Lord Macartney and the present Duke of Northumberland. The Russian service not being suited to his inclinations, and offering but a small field to his ambitious mind, he came to India when Lord Macartney was governor at Madras, and was strongly recommended by Earl Percy to Mr. Hastings. After a variety of adventures he was taken into the service of Madajee Scindiah, in 1784, at the suggestion of Mr. Anderson, the English resident at his court, who procured him permission to raise and discipline two battalions, according to European tactics. This was the origin of his greatness; and when Mr. Anderson introduced De Boigue to Scindiah, he could never have contemplated the danger and trouble which his talents and ambition were destined to occasion to the British Government.—*See an account of this person in the Asiatic Register for* 1804.

who gradually organized and disciplined a military establishment, which was placed under his command, and regularly paid from the revenues of certain districts, allotted by Scindiah for that purpose *. Additional battalions were quickly enrolled, founderies for cannon established, numbers of officers, French as well as English, admitted; and, in short, this army became, in the space of a few years, so formidable, and so complete, as to secure the ascendancy of Scindiah over the other chiefs of the Mahratta confederacy †. He no longer respected the supremacy of the Peishwah, and his views were known to be directed towards the government of the Mahratta empire.

A friendly, but distant, intercourse had subsisted between the British Government and the court of Poonah, since the treaty of Salbhye until 1789, when the aggressions of Tippoo Sultaun rendering war unavoidable, it was the wish of the Marquis Cornwallis, to strengthen the bonds of affinity between the

* India Papers, Malcolm's History.

† Notes on Mahratta War, Asiatic Register, and Malcolm's Political History of India.

two nations. Overtures were accordingly made by Sir Charles Mallett, then resident with the Peishwah, to Nana Furnavese, who, anxious to avenge* the injuries his master had sustained from the Sultaun, consented to conclude an offensive and defensive treaty with the British Government and the Nizam. The most important articles of this treaty, which was signed at Poonah on the 1st of June, 1790, were, that the united forces of the Peishwah and the Nizam should immediately invade the territories of Tippoo, that the Peishwah's army should be joined by two of the Company's battalions; that, if required, he and the Nizam should furnish ten thousand horse to be attached to the English forces; that, in the event of defeat, every effort should be made by the one to relieve the other; and that, in case of success, an equal division should be made of the conquered territories, attention being paid to the convenience of the parties, relative to their respective frontiers; that the southern jagheers should be made over to the Nizam and the Peishwah respectively; that

---

* Malcolm.

peace should only be made by mutual consent: and that if, after the conclusion of peace, Tippoo should molest or attack either of the contracting parties, the others should assist in repelling the insult *.

Madajee Scindiah was not a party to the treaty † of Poonah, for this ambitious chief had long beheld, with an anxious eye, the increasing preponderance of England; and, alarmed at approaching danger, endeavoured to provide for his own safety by counteracting our measures. The terms of the treaty were, however, adhered to by Nana Furnavese, and a body of horse under Hurry Punt, accompanied Lord Cornwallis to Seringapatam; while another party under Purseram Bhow, joined three battalions ‡ of Sepoys, and sat down before Darwar, which surrendered after a siege of twenty-nine weeks §.

---

* Indian Treaties.

† This treaty consisted in all of fourteen articles, and was ratified by the Governor General, on the 5th of July, 1790.

‡ These battalions were commanded by Colonel Frederick; and afterwards, in consequence of the death of that gallant officer, by Captain Little. They were landed in the Conkan, whence they marched to Darwar.

§ Major Moor, who accompanied this detachment, has published an interesting narrative of its proceedings. The

The Peishwah was a party to the treaty of Seringapatam, which concluded this war, and he received, as his share of the spoils taken from Tippoo, the countries of Darwar and Savanore, with territory yielding in all a revenue of about five lacks of pagodas *.

An hereditary enmity had always subsisted between the court of Poonah and the Nizam, and, although they had, at times, acted in union, the remembrance of ancient wrongs, the contiguity of their frontiers, the unsettled demand for choute, and the restless and rapacious spirit of the Mahrattas, tended to keep alive their mutual rancour †. The intimate connexion between the British Government and the Nizam augmented this animosity on the part of the Mahrattas, and excited the fears of Scindiah, who now presided over the councils of Poonah ‡. The views of this distinguished soldier insensibly expanded with the success of his arms; and there is reason to believe, that he latterly cherished those

---

greater proportion re-embarked at Cannanore, while a small party returned to Bombay, by the route of Beejepoor and Poonah.

* India Papers.—Malcolm. † MSS.

‡ India Papers.—Malcolm.

ambitious schemes which were entertained by Bajeerow previous to the battle of Paniput. But as the power of the Company was the principal barrier to the accomplishment of his designs, his thoughts were naturally bent on lessening that influence which they had lately acquired by their victories over Tippoo, and the establishment of a subsidiary force with the Nizam. Scindiah had expressed his dissatisfaction at the treaty of Poonah, he courted the alliance of the sultaun *; and his influence with Nana Furnavese prevented that minister from signing a treaty of guarantee, which the Marquis Cornwallis was so anxious to conclude before his return to Europe†. The Nizam was, however, the immediate object of attack; and it is to be regretted that the British Government did not make an effort, to save a faithful ally, from the vengeance of his bitterest enemies.

Madajee Scindiah did not, however, live to see his plans brought to maturity; he died in 1794, and his power devolved on his nephew, Dowlut Row, who inherited the ambition, but not the judgment or talents of

---

* India Papers. † Malcolm.

his uncle. His death, therefore, did not suspend the preparation for a war, or make any apparent alteration in the sentiments of the Peishwah's ministers. Dowlut Row Scindiah drew a great part of his army from Hindostan, and in 1795 marched against the Nizam, who advanced from Bedur to meet him. An action was fought, which was followed by the retreat of the Nizam, who fell back upon Kurdlah *; where, allowing himself to be shut up and deprived of supplies, he was compelled to sign a convention, by which he admitted all the claims of the Mahrattas, agreed to cede to them the fort and district of Dowlutabad, to pay three crores of rupees, and to deliver Azeem ool Omrah, his prime minister, into the hands of Nana Furnavese, as a hostage for the fulfilment of the convention †. From Kurdlah, the Nizam returned to Hyderabad, and Scindiah commenced his march to Oujein, but before he had time to reach

* A fort in the Deckan, surrounded on three sides by hills, and open to the west by a pass, which on this occasion was immediately occupied by the Mahratta army.—*Malcolm.*

† Two battalions of females are said to have accompanied the Nizam, in this campaign, and to have been the principal cause of his disgrace.

that capital, the death of Madhoo Row, offered a new subject of dispute, and eventually involved the Mahratta country in a civil war.

The celebrated Ragobah, who from the conclusion of the treaty of Salbhye until his death, resided at the town of Cowpergoug, on the banks of the Godaverry, left two sons, Bajeerow and Chimnajee Appah ; who, on the decease of their father, were removed, by the orders of Nana Furnavese, to the fortress of Juneer in the vicinity of Poonah.—There is some mystery in the event that caused the release of these princes, but it is generally believed that the young Peishwah, anxious to alleviate the sufferings of his cousins, opened a correspondence with Bajeerow; Nana Furnavese having, however, intercepted some of the letters, upbraided his master in so unbecoming a manner, that the latter, unable to revenge the insult, threw himself in despair from the battlements of his palace and was killed on the spot*. Bajeerow, the eldest son of Ragobah was the next of blood, and presumptive heir to the musnud, but his

* See Tone's Letters.

elevation was at first opposed by Nana Furnavese, who could not expect to retain his authority in the event of Bajeerow's succession to the office of Peishwah. Recourse was therefore had to every expedient and every species of intrigue, to frustrate the expectations of the young prince; nor was it until Scindiah declared his intentions of supporting the claims of Bajeerow, and made a movement towards Juneer, that Nana caused the two brothers to be brought to Poonah, and placed under the protection of Purseram Bhow*. Scindiah encamped on the banks of the Beemah, the son of Ragobah was placed on the throne, and nothing was wanting to his inauguration but the khelaut, which could not be procured without the sanction of Nana, who had removed with the public treasure to Suttarah, where he employed himself in assembling an army. Scindiah from some cause or other, not exactly known, soon betrayed a disposition inimical to Bajeerow, and in conjunction with some of the other chiefs placed the person of the young prince, and nominal heir of the empire, in re-

* Tone.

straint, whilst he invested his younger brother Chimnajee Appah * with the ensigns of office, and raised Purseram Bhow to the situation of Dewan, or Regent †.

Bajeerow was at first treated with politeness, and even respect, by Scindiah, his confinement was not severe, and he was allowed the attendance of his own servants ‡; but his enemies being afterwards desirous of sending him to the fortress of Asseerghur, every effort was tried to induce him to consent to his removal. These endeavours proved long ineffectual, but the necessities of nature could not be resisted, and the want

* The young prince, who was only eleven years of age, refused to usurp his brother's rights, and was so incensed at the conduct of Purseram Bhow and Scindiah, that he attempted to destroy himself.

† Tone's Letters.

‡ A strong party, at the head of which was the Maun Blyes (a sort of grand council, composed of the chief men of the empire, and nominally at the head of the military force); and Tukojee Holkar secretly favoured his cause, and the quarrels of the new ministry offered a fair opportunity of carrying their plans into execution; but either from treachery, or a want of confidence in each other, their plans fell to the ground. These were Purseram Bhow, Ballajee Tantia, the minister of Scindiah, and Bapoo Firhia, the hereditary standard-bearer.

of food compelled him to request that he might be sent to Jamjerry *. He remained in that fortress for about five months, at the termination of which period another revolution drew him from his prison, and restored him to his rights. The chief mover and instigator of the revolution was Nana Furnavese, who, besides commanding an army in the Conkan, had his agents at work in every part of the capital, and even in the camps of his enemies. The genius of this singular person seemed as if moulded by nature purposely to acquire and maintain an ascendency over his countrymen; and although at a distance, his influence was such as to render nugatory the acts of the Regent, and to hurl the thunder intended for his own destruction upon the heads of his enemies †.

---

* He was put in Dherna, that is to say, he was compelled to remain in the same spot without food or water for two days; and Scindiah, as a point of honour, continued in the same situation for the same length of time. This was, however, repeated with Bajeerow, until he was brought to the verge of the grave.—*Tone.*

† Purseram Bhow, the chief of the Putwurden family, and Jagheerdar of Meritch, was for many years one of the most distinguished commanders of the Poonah state, but he was deficient in those qualifications which were necessary for

Scindiah, Holkar, and Azeem ool Omrah, were at the head of an army, collected for the purpose of driving him from the Conkan, and dispersing his troops ; but he had the address to sow the seeds of dissension amongst his enemies, and to gain over first the Azeem ool Omrah*, and afterwards Scindiah, to his cause. The Bhow was forced to abandon the reins of government, and fly with the young Peishwah to Juneer, where he was besieged, defeated, and taken prisoner †. Bajeerow was again placed on the musnud, but his court was torn by the factions of Scindiah and Nana Furnavese, until the great power of the former triumphed

---

the performance of the duties of his new station, or for holding in subjection so incongruous a mass of turbulence, intrigue, and duplicity, as was to be found in the different members of the government, at the head of which he found himself placed.

* To secure the services of this minister, the three crores of rupees to be paid by the Nizam, in conformity with the terms of the convention of Kurdlah was remitted; and the districts ceded by the same treaty restored.

† He afterwards effected his escape, but was seized, when on his way to Meritch, by the Rajah of Colapore, who ordered him to be cut down in his presence. A deadly feud has, in consequence, subsisted ever since between the two families.

over the talents and wily caution of the latter, and enabled him for several years to trample on the rights of the Peishwah. His pride and ambition could brook no control; he was resolved to possess himself of the whole power of the empire, and the strength and the efficiency of his regular army would have afforded him the means of carrying his plans into execution, had it not been for the successful interference of the Marquis Wellesley.

This nobleman entered upon the government of India in May, 1798, and from the beginning to the end of his career, displayed a degree of ability, vigour, and decision hitherto unparalleled in the annals of the Company. But as it is foreign to the object of this paper to enter into the history of his glorious administration, I shall merely confine myself to that part of his policy, which is more immediately connected with the Mahratta empire. When the reiterated aggressions of Tippoo had again rendered hostilities between him and the British Government inevitable, Lord Wellesley called upon the ministers of the Peishwah to fulfil the conditions of the defensive alliance concluded by Lord Cornwallis. The cautious advice of Nana was overborne by the turbulence of Scindiah *, who had imbibed from his uncle a dread and hatred of the English, and who, instead of affording any assistance in the prosecution of the war, maintained a treacherous correspondence with the Sultaun, even until the fall of Seringapatam †. Lord Wellesley was not unwilling to overlook these hostile measures of the Mahrattas, and anxious to cement the ties of amity between the two states on a surer basis, he offered the Peishwah, under certain conditions, a considerable share of the countries taken from Tippoo. Scindiah, however, not only compelled Bajeerow to decline the offers of the Governor-General, but rejected the overtures which were at the same time made to himself ‡, and was blindly hurried on to acts of the greatest extravagance, not less by his own ambition, than by the advice of the French officers in his service, who were daily acquiring additional

* Notes on the Mahratta War.

† India Papers.

‡ Notes on the Mahratta War.

power and distinction. The regular corps in the service of Scindiah, which had originally been organized by M. de Boigue, was, after the return of that officer to Europe, placed under the command of Monsieur Perran, a Frenchman, whose views were directed to the exclusion of British officers, and to the organization of a military establishment, to be commanded solely by his countrymen *. This army now consisted of about thirty-eight thousand regular infantry, besides cavalry, and a fine train of artillery, supported from the revenue of large territorial possessions, which, as I have before remarked, were expressly allotted for the purpose by Scindiah. These possessions, which extended from the Sutlege through the Punjab, and comprehended a large portion of the Doab, of the Jumna, and the Ganges, including the cities of Agra and Delhi, were placed under the entire management of Monsieur de Perron, and came in direct contact with our north-western frontier. This powerful army, a part of which actually lay encamped in the vicinity of Poonah, enabled

* India Reports.

Scindiah to direct the measures of the Peishwah; but the audacious behaviour of this chief had long given umbrage to the other feudatories of the empire, who trembled for their independence, and who also began to adopt the system of disciplining their troops by European officers.

The most distinguished of these chiefs was Tukojee Holkar, the friend and rival of Madajee Scindiah. Their hereditary jagheers were both situated in the same province, and their possessions were so intermingled with each other, that it is a matter of surprise that each should so long have permitted the other to remain in quiet possession of his territories; and this is the more extraordinary when we reflect on the superior strength of Scindiah, together with the unprincipled and encroaching disposition of the Mahrattas. But on looking into the history of this singular people, we discover so many inconsistencies, and such an accumulation of contradictory measures, that they would seem to set all conjecture and speculation at utter defiance. Holkar died in 1797 *, and left two legitimate sons, Cashy

* Notes on the Mahratta War.

Row and Mulhar Row; and two illegitimate, Eccojee, and the celebrated Jeswunt Row, who had particularly distinguished himself in the action fought at Juneer, against Purserah Bhow. Cashy Row was declared the successor to the territorial possessions of his family * in Malwa; but Mulhar Row claimed an equal division of the country, and disputes running high between the two brothers, they repaired to Poonah, for the purpose of referring their claims to the decision of the Peishwah. Dowlut Row Scindiah, with the view of usurping the estates in dispute, espoused the cause of Cashy Row, and put his younger brother to death. Jeswunt Row and Eccojee, who had attached themselves to the fortunes of Mulhar Row, immediately fled, the one to Nagpoor, the other to Colapoor †. Eccojee was soon afterwards taken, and shared the fate of his unhappy brother; but Jeswunt Row, who, at the instance of Scindiah, had been imprisoned by the Rajah of Berar, found means to escape to Cholea Mehasur, on the

* The possessions were estimated to yield an annual revenue of eighty lacks of rupees.

† Notes on the Mahratta War.

banks of the Nerbudda, where he collected many of the old adherents of his family, and gained several advantages over the troops of Scindiah. This chief pretended to govern the possessions of the Holkar family in the name of Cashy Row *, and, no doubt, would have appropriated their revenues to his own use, had not the two brothers, sensible of his views, agreed to reconcile their differences, as the only means of saving their paternal estates †. A contest, therefore, ensued between Scindiah and Jeswunt Row Holkar, which continued for several years, and in which the superior talents and activity of the latter enabled him successfully to combat the more numerous and efficient armies of his rival and oppressors. These operations had hitherto been confined to Hindostan, when early in the year 1802, Holkar made a sudden movement to the south, and crossing the Narbudda, rapidly advanced upon Poonah, where the influence of his enemy was still predominant ‡. Jeswunt Row having maintained that Kundit

---

* He had also seized upon the infant son of Mulhar Row.

† Notes on the Mahratta War.

‡ Notes on the Mahratta War.

Row, the infant son of his deceased brother, was the head of the family, the alleged motive of his proceeding to Poonah, was to obtain from the Peishwah, as legitimate head of the empire, a decision in his favour, and an order for the liberation of his nephew, whom Scindiah held in confinement. But there is reason to believe that the views of Jeswunt Row were directed to a more important object. He naturally concluded that while he impaired the authority of Scindiah, by the destruction of his ascendency at Poonah, he might subject the Peishwah, who had not the means of opposing him, to admit of his influence instead of that of his rival. Scindiah, who was at Oujein, and not insensible of the dangers likely to arise from the sudden movement of Holkar, sent a reinforcement to Poonah, where it arrived, and formed a junction with the Peishwah's troops in the month of September. Holkar, who had more than once during this struggle, solicited assistance from the British Government, expressed a wish for the mediation of the resident at Poonah, in order to effect an accommodation with the Peishwah; but Bajeerow evinced a determined aversion to such a measure, and never ceased to consider Jeswunt Row as a rebel against the legitimate authority of the empire. An action took place on the 25th of October, in which victory declared for Holkar, who became master of the capital, but failed in his object of seizing the person of the Peishwah *. That prince fled to the sea-coast, near Bancoote, from whence he and his adherents were conveyed in vessels sent by the government of Bombay to Bassein. Bajeerow having thus thrown himself upon the generosity of the British Government, accepted the terms of alliance which had been so frequently proffered to him by the Governor-General, as the only means of liberating himself from the yoke of Holkar and Scindiah †.

It may be readily believed, that the Peishwah must have contemplated the eventual success of either of these chieftains, with equal sentiments of jealousy and distrust; though the contumely which he had already experienced from Scindiah, must have con-

* See Lord Wellesley's Notes on the Mahratta War.

† Notes on the Mahratta War.

vinced him that he had little to expect from that quarter, he had still more to dread from the violence and injustice of Holkar. The evident object of each was to establish his own ascendency on the wreck of the Peishwah's authority; and in his name to secure to themselves the whole civil, as well as military power of the state*. Had Bajeerow inherited any portion of the talents or energy of his forefathers, he would have availed himself of the quarrels of his enemies to collect an army, which he could have done without difficulty; and at its head he might have demanded respect, and exacted that obedience which was due to his situation, as the constitutional head of the empire. But

---

* When the Peishwah had fled from Poonah, it was Holkar's design to place the son of Amrut Row on the Musnud, to make his father Dewan, and himself commander of all the troops; or, in other words, to take the power into his own hands. It is a singular fact, that the Mahrattas have seldom committed any great act of aggression, without using some cloak to hide its enormity; they conquered and held Hindostan in the name of the Great Mogul: Scindiah's violent and unjust proceedings were sanctioned by the Peishwah's authority, and the Peishwah himself acted as the minister of the Rajah of Suttarah. Instances of this kind are to be found in every period of the Mahratta history.

though possessed of good natural talents, his indolence and excessive timidity rendered him unfit for so spirited a line of conduct, and made him the convenient tool of every usurping chief and intriguing bramin. The prince, who from his earliest infancy had been exposed to the vicissitudes of fortune, found himself now reduced to the necessity of choosing either to remain as the pageant of Holkar or Scindiah, or of accepting the terms of a foreign alliance, which he was aware would lead to a total annihilation of his political independence. The fate of Tippoo, and the state of humiliating dependance to which the Nizam had been reduced by the acceptance of our subsidiary force were always present to his imagination or sounded in his ears, by those who were near him; and we may conclude that it was not without great reluctance that he consented to the treaty of Basseim. This treaty was signed by Colonel Close *, on the 31th of December, and on the 13th of April, the Peishwah returned to his capital, which had been previously taken possession

* The late Sir Barry Close, a most able and distinguished officer, and one of the greatest ornaments of an army, in which he had served for thirty-five years of his life.

of by a party of British troops, under the command of Major-Gen. Wellesley*.

It was stipulated by the treaty of Basseim, that the friends and enemies of either should be the friends and enemies of both; and that all former treaties and agreements between the two states, then in force, and not contrary to the tenor of the new engagement, should be confirmed by it. That the British Government should not permit any power or state whatsoever, to commit with impunity, any act of unprovoked hostility or aggression, against the rights and territories of the Peishwah. That his highness should receive a permanent subsidiary force, of not less than six thousand regular native infantry, with the usual proportion of field pieces and artillery men; for the payment of which, he agreed to cede territories yielding a revenue of twenty-six lacks of rupees. That the subsidiary force should at all times be ready to execute services of importance; such as the protection of the person of his Highness, his heirs and successors, the chastisement of rebels or exciters of disturbances, and the due correction of such of his

* Notes on the Mahratta War.

subjects or dependents who might withhold the payment of the circar's just claims; but it was not to be employed on trifling occasions; nor to be stationed in the country, to collect the revenues, nor against any of the principal branches of the Mahratta empire, nor in levying contributions, like Moolkgeeree, from Mahratta dependents.

The Peishwah relinquished all the rights, claims, and privileges of the Mahratta state affecting the city of Surat, in consideration of which, the Company agreed that a piece of land, yielding a sum equal in value to the said claims, should be deducted from the districts ceded by his Highness. His Highness agreed, in the event of war breaking out between the English and any European nation, to discharge from his service and expel from his dominions, all Europeans whose sentiments were known to be hostile to the British interests. The Peishwah engaged never to commit any act of personal hostility and aggression against his highness the Nizam, or any of the Honourable Company's allies or dependents, or against any of the principal branches of the Mahratta empire; and in the event of differences arising, to abide by the arbitration of the British Government. That the unsettled disputes which had long subsisted between the courts of Poonah and Hyderabad, should be amicably adjusted by the British Government; and with this view his Highness agreed to conform to the stipulations of the treaty of Mahar, and that the Nizam should be exempted from the payment of choute. His Highness acknowledged the previous engagements of the Company with the Guickwar, and that the British Government should examine into, and finally adjust the unsettled accounts between that prince and the Poonah state. That in the event of war, the Peishwah should furnish five thousand cavalry and three thousand infantry, with a due proportion of ordnance and military stores, and such further force as he should be able to bring into the field. The Peishwah engaged neither to commence nor to pursue any negotiations with any power whatever, without previously consulting with the British Government; and the Honourable Company agreed not to interfere with his Highness's children, relations, subjects, or servants. That, in the event of disturbances at any time occurring in the districts ceded to the Company by this treaty, his Highness was to permit a proportion of the subsidiary force to be employed in the restoration of tranquillity; and in like manner, should any disturbances break out in any part of his Highness's dominions, contiguous to the Company's frontier, the government should despatch such of its troops, as might be most conveniently stationed, to the disturbed quarter*.

* Indian Treaties.

CHAP IV.

IT neither was, nor could be contemplated, that the great predatory chieftains of the empire, would approve of a treaty which baffled all their hopes of future aggrandisement; and not only gave the British Government a right of interference in their concerns, but introduced a large body of foreign troops into the centre of their country. Scindiah, Holkar, and the Rajah of Berar, suspending their mutual animosities, formed a league, and agreed to support each other in subverting the alliance formed by the treaty of Bassein. With this view, the combined armies of Scindiah and the Bhonslah drew towards the south; and occupying a threatening position on the immediate frontier of the Nizam's dominions, clearly demonstrated their hostile * intentions. After many months spent in

* Notes on the Mahratta War.

fruitless negotiations, in which the ministers of Scindiah had recourse to all the systematic cunning and evasion, so conspicuous in Mahratta diplomacy, the British resident quitted their camp, and war was declared between the Company and the confederates. The geographical situation of Scindiah's territories, his ambition, his inveterate hatred of the English, and the magnitude, as well as efficiency of the regular force, which, under his general M. Perron, occupied a tract of fertile country, immediately adjoining our most valuable frontier, had long rendered him a very suspicious, and even dangerous neighbour. The sagacity of Lord Wellesley, duly appreciated this danger; and it was principally with a view to guard against the evils which were to be apprehended from his ambition and power, that the Governor-General so anxiously pressed the treaty of Bassein.

It would be superfluous to give any detailed narrative of the memorable events of a war, which first gave scope to the talents of the greatest general of the age, and placed the empire of Hindostan, with a population of sixty millions of souls, at the absolute disposal of a small and distant island of the Atlantic.

The exploits of Wellesley and Lake, and the glorious battles of Delhi, and Laswarre, of Assaye and Argœum, destroyed the power and scattered armies of the confederates, who, in the short space of a few months, lost the fairest portion of their dominions, the whole of their artillery and military stores, and the strongest of their fortresses *. Hurled in an instant from the pinnacle of power, they lay prostrate at the feet of the British Government, who granted them peace on better terms than they had a right to expect, or the behaviour of Scindiah had merited †. Both these treaties were negotiated and concluded by Sir A. Wellesley, with a degree of promptitude and decision, which has on every occasion characterized the conduct of this illustrious officer. On the 16th of June, the Rajah of Berar sued for peace, on the 17th the treaty was signed, and on the 14th of July, 1804, ratified by the Governor-General.

By this treaty the Rajah engaged to cede to the Honourable Company and their allies,

* Malcolm.

† They separately sued for peace, and neither the one or the other deemed it necessary to be guided by the opinion nor determination of his ally.

the province of Cuttack, including the port and district of Balasore*, and all the territories of which he had collected the revenues, in participation with the Nizam, and of which he had possession to the westward of the Wurdah. It was agreed that the river Wurdah, from its issue in the Jujardy-hills, to its junction in the Godaverry, should be the western boundary of the Nagpoor territories. The hills, on which the forts of Narvulla and Gawelghur are situated, to remain in the possession of the Rajah; whilst every thing to the south of those hills, and west of the Wurdah, was to belong to the British Government and its allies. The Rajah of Berar, for himself, his heirs, and successors, renounced all claims on the territories of the British Government and their allies; and the Honourable Company engaged to arbitrate all disputes and differences between the Nizam, the Rajah of Berar, and the Peishwah. The Rajah engaged never to take or retain in his service, the subject of any European or American power, without the consent of the British Government; the Honour-

* A town in the province of Cuttack, one hundred and ten miles S. W. of Calcutta.

able Company agreeing in return, not to give any aid or countenance to any discontented relation, or other subjects of the Rajah, who might fly from or rebel against his authority. It was stipulated that accredited ministers from each should reside at the court of the other; and the Rajah, renouncing all adherence to the confederacy formed by him with the other Mahratta chiefs, engaged not to assist those chiefs, if the war with them should still continue *.

The treaty with Scindiah immediately followed that of the Rajah of Berar, and was signed and concluded in the English camp at Surje Aujengaum, on the 30th of December, and ratified by Scindiah on the 5th of January, 1803.

By this treaty, the Maha Rajah ceded to the Honourable Company and their allies, all his forts, territories and rights in the Doab of Jumna and the Ganges, as well as his possessions in the countries to the northward of Jyepoor, Joudpoor, and Gohud. He also ceded to the Company and their allies, the fort and territory of Baroach, the fort and

---

* Indian Treaties.

territory of Ahmed-nuggur, and all the territories to the south of the Adjunte Hills, and all other districts between that range of hills and the Godaverry. He renounced all claims of every description upon the British Government, the Nizam, the Peishwah, and the Guickwar. The other forts and territories conquered from him during the war were restored; and in order that no individual might suffer in consequence of this arrangement, the Company agreed to pay pensions or grant lands in Jagheer, to certain of Scindiah's Surdars, to the amount of seventeen lacks of rupees. Certain treaties made by the British Government with the Rajahs and others, tributary to Scindiah, were confirmed, their independence acknowledged, and no person whatever was to be molested on account of the part he might have taken during the war. Scindiah renounced all claims upon his majesty Shah Allum, and engaged never again to interfere in his affairs. He also agreed never to take or retain in his service, any Frenchman, or the subject of any European or American power, the government of which being at war with the British Government, or any British subject, without the consent of the Company*.

* Indian Treaties.

Such were the principal stipulations of this treaty, but some disputes having afterwards arisen regarding the fortress of Gwalior, the bonds of union were strengthened by a new treaty of defensive alliance, concluded by Colonel Malcolm, at Boorhanpoor, in the month of February, 1804.

By this it was stipulated, that the friends and enemies of either state, should be the friends and enemies of both: and the British Government engaged never to permit any power whatsoever, to commit with impunity, any act of unprovoked hostility or aggression, against the rights and territories of Scindiah; and with a view of fulfilling this treaty, the Maha Rajah agreed to receive from the Company, a subsidiary force of six thousand infantry, with the usual proportion of artillery, to be paid by the Honourable Company out of the produce of the revenues of the territories, ceded by Scindiah by the treaty of Surje Aujengaum. The subsidiary force to be employed in the same manner as that with the Peishwah. The Maha Rajah further engaged, that he would never employ in his service, or permit to reside in his dominions, any European or American subject, without the acquiescence of the British Government;

which on its part agreed, never to employ or permit to reside in its dominions, any person subject to Scindiah or others, who might be guilty of crimes, or of hostility against the person or government of that prince. The Maha Rajah engaged never to negotiate with any powerful state, without consulting the Company's government; and the latter on their part, declared that they would not interfere in his Highness's internal concerns, nor support any of his relations or dependants, in any act of opposition to his authority, but on the contrary, aid and assist him in the reduction of all such offenders. The Maha Rajah engaged never to commit any act of hostility or aggression, against any state in alliance with the Company; and that in the event of differences arising with other states, he agreed to submit to the arbitration of the Company. In the event of war between the contracting parties and any other state, it was stipulated that the English subsidiary force, joined to six thousand horse belonging to Scindiah, should be put in motion to oppose the enemy; and in addition to this, the contracting parties agreed to furnish as large a force as their dominions could supply, for the prosecution of the war. They engaged mutually to assist each other, in the suppression of disturbances in their respective territories; and any disputes that might afterwards arise between the Peishwah and Scindiah, were to be adjusted by the British Government, on the principles of truth and justice *.

Of the territories, ceded by these treaties to the British Government and its allies, the country belonging to the Rajah of Berar to the west of the Wurdah, and south of the hills of Namulla and Gwalghur, together with those Pergunnahs, of which the revenues had formerly been collected by the Bhonslah Rajah, in participation with the Soubahdar of the Deckan, were made over in perpetual sovereignty to his Highness the Nizam, with the exception of certain districts reserved to the Nagpoor state by the 5th article of the treaty of Deogaum. The territory to the south of the Adjunte Hills, including the town and district of Jaulna, and all other districts between that range of hills and the Godaverry, were also given to the Nizam; whilst the fort, city, and district of Ahmed-

* Indian Treaties.

nuggur, were ceded to the dominions of his Highness the Peishwah*.

The successful termination of this war in so very short a period, and the rapid succession of triumphs which every where attended the British arms, must in justice be attributed to the bold and masterly measures, adopted by the Marquis Wellesley, and the energy with which they were carried into effect by the able and distinguished officers, whom he had selected for that purpose. The superior quality and efficiency of the troops which were brought to bear at once on every part of the enemy's territory, confounded the efforts of the confederates, who, struck with terror and amazement, were unable to make any effectual resistance. The result of this war removed all danger of a French ascendency in Hindostan, and gave us possession of the person and capital of the Mogul; while Scindiah, deprived of his conquests and military resources, almost sunk into the condition of a mere predatory chief.

Holkar, who had retired into Hindostan, regarded with apparent apathy, and, per-

* Indian Treaties.

haps, with some satisfaction, the destruction of his rival; and, although he had promised to become a party to the league, he made no efforts to assist his allies. But no sooner had the downfal of Scindiah been accomplished, than he unveiled his designs, and, in reply to a communication from the Governor-General, requesting him to retire into his own dominions, he made the most insolent and extravagant demands, threatening at the same time, in the event of refusal, that he would ravage and destroy the Company's territories *. . His menaces were followed by acts of open aggression; he openly solicited aid from the other predatory powers, and commenced hostilities, by ordering his troops to plunder the country of Jyepoor. The result of this war, although chequered with some considerable failures, proved in the end equally fatal to Holkar as that of 1803 had to Scindiah. His army, which, at the commencement of the campaign, amounted

* His demands were, that he should be permitted to collect the choute agreeably to the custom of his ancestors. That all possessions formerly held by his family should be given up to him; and that his country should be guaranteed to him.—*Malcolm.*

to forty thousand horse, twenty thousand infantry, and about a hundred pieces of cannon, did not, at its termination, exceed fifteen thousand horse, and twenty pieces of artillery*. At Deig, at Fultyghur, he had suffered two memorable defeats; the former deprived him of his infantry and artillery, and the latter had broken the spirit of his cavalry, but he still maintained the contest for upwards of a year; when, driven beyond the Hyphasis †, he was compelled to sue for peace, which was concluded in December, 1805, on terms that left him in the possession of the territories of his family, in Malwa and Candeish, but obliged him to resign all claim on the country of the Tonk Rampoora, in Hindostan ‡. The unexpected

* See Malcolm's Political History of India.

† Now called the Sutlege, one of the rivers of the Punjab, and the eastern boundary of the province of Lahore. It has its source in the mountains of Hymalya, and after forming a junction with the Beyah, enters the Indus below the Moultain. The combined stream of the Sutlege and Beyah is the ancient Hyphasis, and is a large and navigable river, many miles above its junction with the Indus.—*For an excellent account of the rivers of the Punjab, see Elphinstone's Cabul.*

‡ By the treaty with Juswunt Row Holkar, which was

recall of Marquis Wellesley, before he had contemplated those plans for the permanent

---

signed on the 24th of December, 1805, that chieftain renounced all right and title to Tonk Rampoora, Boondie, and all other places north of the Boondie Hills, then occupied by the British Government. The Honourable Company engaged to have no concern with the ancient possessions of the Holkar family, in Newar, Malwa and Harowtee, or with any of the Rajahs situated to the south of the Chumbul, and to deliver over such of the ancient possessions of the Holkar family, in the Deckan, as were then in possession of the Company, with the exception of Chandore, Ambar, and Sengham, and some pergunnahs to the south of the Godaverry, all of which were to be returned to him at the expiration of eighteen months, in the event of his conduct being such as to satisfy the British Government of his amicable intentions. Holkar renounced all claims, of every description, in the province of Bundelcund; but in the event of his conduct being satisfactory, the Company agreed, at the expiration of two years, to give the district of Coonch, in Jagheer, to the daughter of Holkar, who, at the same time, renounced every claim upon the British Government and its allies. He also engaged never to entertain any European in his service, without the consent of the British Government; and upon those conditions he was permitted to return unmolested to Hindostan.

By a declaratory article of this treaty, the provisions of the second article of the treaty was declared void, and the district of Tonk Rampoora, and such other districts in its vicinity as were formerly in possession of his family, were restored to Holkar.

security of the British possessions in India, which his powerful mind had always contemplated, may, in truth, be said to have deprived us of the full harvest of our triumphs. The great solicitude for peace felt by his immediate successors, and their declared anxiety to adhere to a system of strict neutrality, roused the drooping spirits of the Mahratta chiefs *. Large concessions were made to Scindiah, his treatment of the British resident was overlooked, and his claims on Gwalior and Gohud, admitted in a new treaty, concluded with him at Mustaphapoor, on the 22d of November, 1805 †.

* Sammulpoor and Patna were also restored to the Rajah of Berar.

† The treaty of Surje Aujengaum, with the following exceptions, were to remain binding between the two states. The Company, from considerations of friendship, agreed to cede to the Maha Rajah the fortress of Gwalior, and such parts of the territory of Gohud, as were described in an accompanying schedule; and in return for this cession, Scindiah relinquished all claim to the pensions of fifteen lacks of rupees, granted to some of his chiefs, by an article in the treaty of Surje Aujengaum.—The Maha Rajah agreed to cede to the Company all the territory north of the river Chumbal, which was ceded to him by the 7th article of the

Jeswunt Row Holkar was permitted to return to Malwa, the estate of his family, including Tonk Rampoora*, and other fertile districts on the north of the Chumbul, were restored; and at the conclusion of a war, which had cost the Company so much blood and treasure, and in which he had been

---

treaty of Surje Aujengaum; and the Company renounced their claims to the possessions on the south bank of that river, with the exception of the talooks of Bhadeck and Soorseperah; the Honourable Company agreed to grant the Maha Rajah the annual sum of four lacks of rupees, and to assign, within their territories in Hindostan, a jagheer, yielding a revenue of two lacks of rupees, to Baezah Bhye, the wife of Scindiah; and another jagheer, amounting to one lack of rupees, to the daughter of that chief. The Company further engaged to enter into no treaty with the Rajahs of Oudipoor and Jandpoor, and Kootah, or other chiefs, tributaries of Dowlut Row Scindiah, situated in Malwa, Mecvar, or Marwar, and in no shape whatever, to interfere with the settlement which Scindiah might make with those chiefs. The Company engaged not to restore to Jeswunt Row Holkar any of the possessions of his family, lying between the Tapti and Chumbul, which might have been taken by Scindiah; nor would the Company's government concern itself with any arrangements which Scindiah might make to the family of Holkar, nor take part in any dispute, or war, which might result from such arrangement or settlement.—*Indian Treaties.*

* A rich district in Ajmere.

completely vanquished, Holkar found himself in much the same situation as at its commencement, with this remarkable exception, that his claims to the usurped dominions of his brother were tacitly admitted by the British Government. The engagements with the Rajpoot Princes and other chiefs who had assisted Lord Lake during the war, and who placed the most implicit confidence in our faith, were dissolved, and numerous bodies of irregular troops who had been received into our service, and were inhabitants of the provinces we had conquered, were turned loose without the means of subsistence *. The consequences which were apprehended as likely to arise from this change of policy †, have actually come to pass; and the peace of India has been violated by an organized association of freebooters, who, under the denomination of Pindaries, have lately be-

* The armies of Holkar and Scindiah were chiefly composed of Rajpoots and Mahomedans; most of whom, in the opinion of Lord Lake, might have been detached from their predatory habits and rendered useful subjects.

† See Malcolm's Political History of India, where this subject is most ably, and if I might use the expression, prophetically treated.

come the scourge and terror of the neighbouring countries.

Numberless causes may be assigned for the surprising increase of the Pindaries. The great chieftains of the Mahratta confederacy have severely felt, and will never recover, from the effects of their defeat; the destruction of his regular army and deranged finance, have lessened Scindiah's means of preserving order in his dominions; and the country between the Nerbudda and the Jumna, has consequently relapsed into that state of barbarism, from which it had in some measure emerged during the latter years of the reign of Madajee Scindiah. The ill-timed and impolitic dismissal of the irregular troops from our service, at the conclusion of Holkar's war in 1806, the silent operation of our subsidiary system, which has induced the Princes of the Deckan to discharge their armies, and above all, the nature and principles of the Mahratta government have contributed to aggravate an evil, which merits the most serious and attentive consideration of the British Government.

These dangers were foreseen, and in 1805 when Holkar was driven from Hindostan, the obvious necessity of adopting some arrangement which might prevent the military classes, thrown out of employment, from becoming desperate, was earnestly recommended by a distinguished officer of the Company's Service*; but these suggestions were not attended to, either from a pressure of financial difficulties, or from an idea that the British interests might be promoted†, instead of endangered by the continued contests of these banditti, and of the predatory powers unconnected with the British Government.

---

* Vide Colonel Malcolm's Letters. A. D. 1803 and 1805.

† Vide Public Correspondence, 1805-6.

CHAP. V.

THE name of Pindarie may be found in Indian History* as early as the commencement of the last century; several bands of these freebooters followed the Mahratta armies in their early wars in Hindostan, and they are mentioned by Ferishta as having fought against Zoolfeccar Khan, and the other generals of Aurengzebe. One of their first and most distinguished leaders was a person named Ponapah, who ravaged the Carnatic and took Vellore early in the reign of Sahoojee. This chief is said to have been succeeded by Chingody and Hool Sewar, who commanded fifteen thousand horse at the battle of Paniput, and under whom the Pindarie system would seem to have assumed a more regular form. They were divided into Durrahs, or tribes, commanded by Sirdars or

* MSS.

chiefs; people of every country, and of every religion*, were indiscriminately enrolled in this heterogeneous community, and a horse and sword were deemed sufficient qualifications for admission†. A common interest kept them united; the chiefs acquired wealth and renown in the Mahratta wars, they seized upon lands which they were afterwards tacitly permitted to retain, and transmitted with their estates, the services of their adherents to their descendants.

Heeroo and Burran are subsequently mentioned as leaders‡ of the Pindaries; and in order to distinguish the followers of Tuckojee Holkar from those of Madajee Scindiah, they were henceforward denominated the Scindiah Shahee§, and the Holkar Shahee.

---

* No great religious enmity would ever appear to have existed between the Mahrattas and Mahomedans. The same language is common to them both, many of their customs are the same, and the former have adopted many of the titles of the latter. The generals of Scindiah and the other Mahratta chiefs, are often Mahomedans; and Bramins frequently govern the courts of Mussulmen princes.

† MSS.

‡ MSS.

§ They are still termed so, and it may be translated, Scindiah our King, or Supporters of Scindiah's Rule.

Dost Mohummud and Ryan Khan, the sons of Heeroo are still powerful chiefs; but in an association which is daily augmented by the admittance of strangers, it is natural to suppose that influence will not be confined to hereditary claims, and that men of superior genius and enterprise will ultimately rise to the chief command. This is accordingly found to be the case, and Seetoo, who is now the most powerful of all the Pindarie leaders, was a few years ago a person of no consideration. It is only of late, that these banditti have become really formidable, and they may now be looked upon as an independent power, which if properly united, under an able commander, would prove the most dangerous enemy that could arise to disturb the peace and prosperity of India.

The climate and hardy habits of these plunderers render tents or baggage an unnecessary incumbrance; each person carries a few days' provisions for himself and for his horse, and they march for weeks together, at the rate of thirty and forty miles a day, over roads and countries impassable for a regular army. They exhibit a striking resemblance to the Cossacks, as well in their customs as in the activity of their movements. Their arms are the same, being a lançe and a sword, which they use with admirable dexterity; their horses, like those of the Cossacks, are small, but extremely active; and they pillage, without distinction, friends as well as foes. They move in bodies seldom exceeding two or three thousand men, and hold a direct undeviating course until they reach their destination, when they at once divide into small parties, that they may with more facility plunder the country, and carry off a larger quantity of booty; destroying, at the same time, what they cannot remove. They are frequently guilty of the most inhuman barbarities, and their progress is generally marked by the smoking ruins of villages, the shrieks of women, and the groans of their mutilated husbands. At times they wallow in abundance, while at others they cannot procure the common necessaries of life; and their horses, which are trained to undergo the same privations as their masters, often receive a stimulus of opium when impelled to uncommon exertion. Night and the middle of the day are dedicated to repose; and recent experience* has shewn us that they may be surprised with effect at such hours. Fighting is not their object, they have seldom been known to resist the attack even of an inferior enemy; if pursued, they make marches of extraordinary length, and if they should happen to be overtaken, they disperse, and re-assemble at an appointed rendezvous; or if followed into their country, they immediately retire to their respective homes. Their wealth and their families are scattered over that mountainous tract of country which borders the Nerbudda† to the north. They find protection either in castles belonging to themselves, or from those powers with whom they are either openly or secretly connected. They can scarcely be said to present any point of attack, and the defeat or destruction of any particular chief, would only effect the ruin of an individual, without removing the evil of a system equally in-

---

* This is a custom also practised by the Usbeck Tartars, and Turkomans, whose horses are much superior, and perform far more wonderful journeys than those of the Pindaries.

† The Vindhya mountains, a long and narrow, but lofty, range which extends to the W. nearly as far as the Indus.

veterate in its nature, and extensive in its influence.

The most powerful of the Pindarie chiefs are Kurreem Khan, Cheetoo (or Seetoo, as he is often called) and Dost Mohummud. There are, however, several subordinate chiefs, who are the commanders of dhurrahs, or tribes, and acknowledge a tacit obedience to one or other of the three great leaders before mentioned.

Kurreem Khan is descended from an ancient Mahomedan family; his early youth was spent in the service of Holkar, which he subsequently quitted for that of Dowlut Row Scindiah; his character and enterprising spirit soon increased the number of his adherents, he enlarged his possessions, partly by grants from Scindiah, and partly by usurpations from the Rajah of Berar and Nabob of Bhopaul, whose dominions he alternately invaded and ravaged. He possessed himself of several fortresses, and, at the termination of the Mahratta war, his power was such as to excite the fears and jealousy of Scindiah, who caused him to be treacherously seized and confined at Gwalior. Here he lingered some years in prison;

after which, having obtained his release by the payment of a ransom, he resumed his former habits, returned amongst his companions, and, in a short time, became as powerful as he had been before. Scindiah, unable to crush him by open force, had once more recourse to treachery, and taking advantage of a quarrel between Kurreem and Seetoo, assisted the latter, who, having overthrown Kurreem in a pitched battle, compelled him to fly for refuge to Ameer Khan, who made him over to Toolsa Bhye, the widow regent of the Holkar family. Kurreem has since escaped, or rather been liberated, and is now at the head of his dhurrah, which amounts to about five thousand horse, and is cantoned near Barseim, in Bhopaul. It is rumoured that he is about to be reconciled to Scindiah, but after what has passed, they can have no confidence in each other.

Cheetoo, who is at present the greatest of all the Pindarie chiefs, enjoys the confidence and favour of Scindiah. He has lately acquired extensive influence; the numbers of his followers daily continue to increase, and, by a late account, he was said to be at the head of twenty thousand horse, a small corps of bad infantry, and a train of twenty ill served guns. He possesses the forts and districts of Sutwass, which run along the northern branch of the Nerbudda to the south of Oujein, and nearly opposite Hindia*.

Dost Mohummud, the son of Heeroo, is entitled from his birth to hold the chief place over all the Pindarie tribes. This person is, however, inferior to Cheetoo, and the troops subject to his command may amount to between ten and twelve thousand horse, a small body of infantry, and a few guns. A party of the adherents of Dost Mohummud, commanded by his brother, Wausil Khan, invaded our provinces, and there is every reason to believe, that they were accompanied by some of the troops of Scindiah. Their camp is at Bagrode †, a short distance to the north-east of Bilseih ‡, a district in Bhopaul.

---

* The capital of a district of the same name in Candeish, on the south side of the Nerbudda, one hundred and sixteen miles south-east from Oujeim.—*Hamilton.*

† Bagrode is situated about halfway between Bilseih and Saugor.

‡ The town of Bilseih is situated in lat. 23° 33′ N., long. 77° 50′ E.—*See Hamilton's Indian Gazetteer.*

The Holkar branch of the Pindaries, is far less formidable than that of Scindiah. Their chief leader is a person named Kawder Buksh; those of inferior note Tookoo and Sahib Khan; and their united strength may be computed at nearly five thousand horse. They are generally cantoned in the vicinity of Kunool and Sohundra*.

The Pindaries may probably amount altogether to between thirty and forty thousand horse; but in a community so subject to constant fluctuations, it is impossible to form any accurate idea of their number, which must vary from day to day according to the caprice of individuals, and the condition of the adjoining countries. Throughout the greater part of the territories of the native powers in central India, the husbandman is seldom permitted to reap the fruits of his labours; his fields are laid waste, his cottage reduced to ashes, and he has no alternative, but that of

---

* One of the most remarkable of the Pindarie leaders, is a person named Sheik Dallah. This chief has only a small number of followers, but his annual incursions to Berar, his attack with a few hundred horse of the garrison of Nagpoor, and his late exploits, place him as first of these freebooters in courage and enterprise.

joining the standard of some lawless chief. Thus the numbers of the Pindaries may be said to increase in the same ratio, as the means of subsistence diminish; hunger goads them on to the work of destruction, and they rejoice in anticipation of the spoils of wealthy countries. Were they permitted to continue their merciless depredations without molestation, the peninsula of India would in time become a desert, and the few inhabitants that survived the general wreck, a band of savage and licèntious robbers. The pastoral tribes of Arabia and Turkey, although sufficiently prone to pillage, where an occasion may offer, are not impelled by such motives of imperious necessity, as the predatory horse of Hindostan; their slender numbers cover extensive countries, and when their flocks have exhausted the pasture of one plain, they move with their families into another. The Pindaries are, on the contrary, confined to a tract of waste land which has become the general rendezvous of every vagabond and outlaw, and whence they issue in desperate bands, in search of the necessaries of life. Some analogy may at first appear to exist between their usages and those of the early

Mahrattas under Sevajee, but on reflection we shall discover an essential difference in many important points. The adherents of Sevajee were warmed by a strong patriotic feeling, they were all of the same religion and country, and were in fact the long oppressed inhabitants of an ancient kingdom, recovering their rights by the expulsion of a depraved and declining government of strangers. The Pindaries are a mere collection of vagrants from various countries and of different castes and religion, brought together from an inability of otherwise procuring the means of subsistence, divided amongst themselves, and ready at all times to desert their leaders, and enter the service of any prince or state who may support them.

The dominions of our allies have ever since the year 1811, been subject to their incursions. In 1814 * they entered the province of Bahar, and threatened Bengal; and in the two following years invaded the British territories under Fort St. George. Passing with the rapidity of lightning through the country of the Nizam, they suddenly broke in upon

* They came close to Meerzapoor.

the defenceless district of Guntoor, and in an instant spread themselves over the face of the country, every where committing the most shocking and wanton atrocities. In 1816 they returned with redoubled numbers, and extending themselves from the coast of the Conkan to that of Orissa, threw the whole southern part of the peninsula into a state of alarm. They again passed without difficulty and without opposition, through the dominions of our allies the Peishwah and the Nizam; carried fire and sword almost from one end to the other of the district of Ganjam, and returned home, laden with the spoil, and stained with the blood of our subjects. In this last expedition, however, several parties of them were overtaken, and we have the satisfaction to know that they were unable to contend against the Company's troops. The success of the troops under Majors Lushington, Macdoual, and Smith, and of the small detachment of sepoys, under the brave Lieutenant Borthwick *, in the southern part of

* This young and promising officer fell a sacrifice to his exertions, and died of fatigue. The following General Order was issued by Sir Thomas Hislop, on the occasion :

"The

India, and the equally brilliant exploits of several officers of the Bengal army, must have a salutary influence in checking the boldness of the Pindaries, give confidence to our own troops, and convince the native powers that we still preserve unsullied, our accustomed superiority in arms. I leave it to my readers, however, to conjecture the effects which successive incursions of this nature are calculated to produce on the fruitful and populous provinces of the Company; the alarm has spread far and wide, and the confidence of our most

---

"The Commander-in-Chief feels it a duty he is anxious to acquit himself of, to record his highest approbation and applause of the conduct of Lieutenant Borthwick of the 2d batt. 2d reg., and the native officers and men of his small but exemplary detachment. It marks the talent, judgment, and persevering spirit of Lieutenant Borthwick, and the discipline, attachment, and patience of the excellent troops, which, with such inadequate numbers, have effected so much essential service, in finally expelling from the Ganjam districts so numerous a body of predatory horse.

"It is in affairs of this kind, that officers, with limited means, have an opportunity of displaying their professional ability, resources, and spirit; and the present instance not only speaks the rising reputation of Lieutenant Borthwick, but places him in the light of those promising officers, who will be useful ornaments to the service, and their profession."

attached subjects has been shaken in the same proportion, as the hopes of the turbulent and disaffected have been awakened. But before I venture on any proposition for the suppression of this growing evil, it will be necessary to take a succinct view of the political state of the different native powers in India.

CHAP. VI.

OUR subsidiary system, which many think has been carried to too great an extent, has certainly been attended with many inconveniences and much serious embarrassment *. The Nizam and the Peishwah, trusting to us for defence, are unwilling to maintain even the quota of troops stipulated by treaty. Large bodies of horse, formerly in their employ, now swell the ranks of the Pindaries; and strange as it may appear, we have been compelled to combat the servants and subjects of the very power, we are bound by our engagements to protect. The ministers at Hyderabad, are daily guilty of such acts of injustice towards the Jagheerdars and Ryots, as in the

* This question, like many others connected with the extraordinary empire we have established in India, must be guided by comparison with other evils resulting from our condition.

end drive the former into revolt, and the latter into exile. These excesses they would scarcely venturé to commit, if deprived of our support; and therefore we incur the whole odium of their vicious measures, while they are permitted to enjoy the fruits of their indiscriminating extortions, and boundless rapacity. The dominions of the Nizam every where exhibit a sad and melancholy picture of the baneful effects of misrule and oppression; vast tracts of fertile land lie waste and unpeopled, agriculture is at a stand, and improvement is not to be expected where a regular system of corruption and violence actuates the members of every station, from the lord to his meanest dependant. The interior of the country is therefore a scene of perpetual tumult and confusion; and the villagers, left totally unprotected, have to trust to themselves alone for defence against the depredations of domestic as well as of foreign marauders.

The government of the present Nizam has some resemblance to that of the late Omdut ool Omrah, (or perhaps a nearer one to the former government of Lucknow); and the corruptness of his court is only to be equalled by the general spirit of licentiousness which pervades every quarter of his capital. In regard to the Nizam himself, he rarely moves beyond the walls of his Haram. He seldom or never holds a public Durbar, attends but little to the affairs of his dominions, and has only once, I am told, quitted the precincts of his palace since the year 1806. He lives almost entirely with women; his business is chiefly transacted by verbal messages communicated by female attendants, and he never goes from one chamber to another, without being followed by four or five women slaves. The Nizam is extremely jealous of his near relations, whom he suspects of designs against his life; and never sees his children except upon the first day of the Mahomedan year. Mooneer ool Moolk, who succeeded Meer Allum, the late minister, enjoys no share of his confidence, and is, in fact, only a nominal minister, the whole of the business being transacted by Chundoo Laul, a Hindoo, who is supported by all the influence of the British Government. The debauched life of the Nizam has enervated his faculties, and totally incapacitated him from holding the reins of government himself. When momentous affairs render it necessary that he should be consulted, he evinces not merely indecision and apathy, but a sullen disinclination to business. Perhaps this feeling is in some degree grounded on disgust at his condition; he is also supposed to have a rooted animosity against us, but who can judge of the motives which influence a mind of such a construction?

The population of the city of Hyderabad amounts to about three hundred thousand souls. It is, and ever has been, a sink of iniquity, where vice has its full sweep, and where the inhabitants are lost to every sense of shame and propriety. Indolent, luxurious, and depraved, they pass whole nights and days in drunkenness, riot, and the vilest debaucheries; the basest crimes have a fixed price, and the life of an enemy may be bargained away for a trifle.

The Nizam's army has undergone a very considerable, though gradual reduction, since the year 1807; and it may now be estimated to amount to about thirty thousand men, who may be generally regarded as unfit for military pur poses, and whom it might be dangerous even to assemble. I do not in this computation include the Russell brigade, or the corps under Captain Davies, because these troops are in fact employed by us, and imposed upon his Highness as a sort of contingent. The Russell brigade consists of two regiments, each of a thousand men, recruited from the Bengal provinces, and disciplined by British officers. They are clothed and armed better than our own sepoys, and their pay, which amounts to about thirty thousand rupees per mensem, is regularly issued from the treasury of the residency *. The corps, organized by Captain Davies, amounts to about five thousand horse, and may in general be depended upon, if led by natives of respectability and enterprise. It is difficult, however, to accomplish this object, as the better classes of Mahomedans have a strong aversion to any thing like an introduction of European tactics. The Nizam has no regular train of artillery, and the few pieces of ordnance which he pos-

* It may, in fact, be termed the redemption of the greatest part of the tribute of seven lacks of rupees which the Company continues to pay the Nizam for the northern Circars, and which the government of Hyderabad have agreed should be in part applied to the support of this efficient body of men.

sesses are badly served, and in point of fact, unfit for use*.

The above is without doubt a very melancholy picture of the state of the Nizam's government. But all political evils are comparative, and we ought attentively to consider what the situation of his country might have been, had we abstained from all interference in his concerns, since it is doubtful whether the grievances originating in a corrupt and depressed court are greater than those occasioned by open revolt or foreign invasion. I will venture to affirm, that had we not granted the Nizam our immediate protection, he would long since have ceased to exist as a sovereign prince. His country would have fallen a prey to the inroads of the Mahrattas, which he was incapable of resisting; and instead of the aid which he afforded us in our

---

* Seven or eight provincial battalions, each about four hundred strong, are also kept up in various parts of the country, and those of Berar are said to be very good. Two of these, commanded by Captain Lyne, are with Salabat Khan, at Ellickpoor; one is in the Namdair districts, one at Nellgoonda, and the others are employed under Mr. Elliot, who has likewise three thousand Mogul horse with him near Barsein, to the north of the Godaverry.

wars with Tippoo and Scindiah, the resources of his dominions might have been turned against us. We were compelled by strong necessity to interfere, and we had no choice but that of acting as we did, or of assuming the direct management of the Nizam's territories; which, at the time our subsidiary treaty was concluded, would have been a measure equally difficult, unjust, and impolitic. The internal disorders were not introduced by us, they existed long before our subsidiary treaties; for corruption, extortion, and injustice, are the common characteristics of all native governments. Let us also reflect on the injuries we might have experienced, had the resources of the Deckan been at the disposal of an able and enterprising enemy; and remember that we are scarcely entitled to argue against any system, unless we are able to shew that another method could have been productive of more good, and have been attended with fewer evils and less danger.

The Peishwah's government is certainly more efficient, and his country in a less pitiable condition than that of the Nizam. This may be ascribed to the difference in the nature of the governments, and in the habits of the people. The Hindoos are more temperate, more industrious, and more enterprising than the Indian Mahomedans, who, perhaps too much alive to a sense of degradation, and unable to reconcile themselves to their fallen state, quickly yield to despondency, and either abandon themselves to sensual enjoyments, or sullenly brood in dejection and silence over their misfortunes. The Mahratta is a being of a more flexible nature; he bends to the storm which he cannot resist, and as his versatile disposition will never permit him to be idle, he is either engaged on plundering expeditions, or in procuring a subsistence by labour or intrigue. It does not appear that any of the chiefs ever exercised any very despotic sway over those whom they governed, and the state has, for that reason, always assumed rather the form of a league, or sort of republic, than of a kingly government. The orders of the Peishwah have of late seldom been attended to by his Jagheerdars, except where he may have possessed sufficient power to insure compliance; and he has therefore often been led rather to conciliate than command obedience; and to treat them more like equals than subjects. Instances of cruelty practised on individuals are not, however, uncommon, and the love of plunder and family feuds frequently urge one chief to carry fire and sword into the country of another; but the Peishwah's rule, upon the whole, is much less grievous, and more patriarchal than that of the Nizam. The Mahratta constitution has, however, no intelligible form; educated in the arts of deceit and evasion, this singular people dislike all regular and direct proceedings, and as a total want of integrity is every where conspicuous, they have a rooted aversion to the introduction of any thing like a general system of jurisprudence. Any change in the customs and opinions of the Mahrattas must, therefore, be slow and progressive; but at the same time, nothing will tend sooner to produce this effect, than the occasional and mild interference of the British Government.

The Peishwah owes his throne to the British Government, who have maintained him upon it in defiance of the most powerful chiefs of the empire, but the character of this prince is artful, timid, and dissolute*. Trusting,

* It is a peculiar trait in the character of this prince, that he is both exact and honest in all his personal pecuniary concerns, never either evading or protracting payment.

like the Nizam, to his English allies for personal safety and protection, he has, until very lately, maintained but few troops, and every district in his country has in consequence been subject to insurrection. That the Peishwah may collect as much revenue as possible, the Serinjammy lands are no longer bestowed on the military classes; but he has hitherto been able to reap little benefit from this unpopular and impolitic measure, since he has not sufficient power to levy the kist. The Jagheerdars of the southern frontier are in a great degree independent of him, and pay but a trifling, if even any tribute; he has long been unable to derive any revenue from his insulated lands in Malwa and Bundelcund, whilst his territories in Guzzerat have involved him in perpetual disputes with the Guickwar.

Although Bajeerow, as I said before, owes his crown, and perhaps his life, to the British Government; recent events proved, beyond a doubt, that this deluded prince entertained sentiments decidedly hostile to the interests of his protectors. His extraordinary affection for Trimbuckjee Dinglia, the assassination of the Guickwar's minister, and his refusal to deliver up the murderer until the subsidiary force had reached the gates of his capital, are events only attributable to infatuation, or to the entertainment of hopes, which could never have been realized. The escape of Trimbuckjee, his master's subsequent conduct in raising troops and putting his fortress into a state of defence, and the hostile feeling which has been excited against the English in every part of his dominions, are matters still more extraordinary; and lead to a conclusion, that the proceedings of the Peishwah were grounded on a confident expectation of succour from other quarters. There is, indeed, room for belief, that his negotiations were not confined to the courts of Holkar and Scindiah, but even extended to the chiefs of the Pindaries. This cowardice and pusillanimity, and the admirable temper and decision of Mr. Elphinstone have, however, combined to defeat every hostile project. The Peishwah, reduced without a blow to submission, has only received forgiveness by the sacrifice of a revenue of thirty-four lacks of rupees; which the wisdom and generosity of Lord Hastings has exclusively applied to raising and paying troops, chiefly irregular horse, for the safety of the possession of the Poonah state—a measure, which in the end will prove as beneficial to the Peishwah, as it is calculated to promote the general interests of the British Government and its allies.

If Scindiah's sentiments were unfriendly to the British Government, previously to the Mahratta war; it can scarcely be expected that his subsequent misfortunes, and the height from which he has fallen, should have engendered a better feeling towards the authors of his ruin. We may, therefore, assume, that his antipathy towards us is not abated, and that he would gladly join in the adoption of any measure, which should open the most distant prospect of lessening our ascendency, or injuring our resources. His whole conduct since 1806, has betrayed such intentions; he has granted the Pindaries an asylum in his dominions, and sedulously fostered their growth, as an instrument for our annoyance; he has encouraged their inroads into our dominions, and secretly rejoiced in their success; his troops have acted with the plunderers, and he has publicly shared in the spoil after their return. The possessions of this chieftain are still sufficiently ample; the death of Holkar, together with the unprotected condition of the Rajpoot states, have allowed him to make considerable addition to his dominions since the peace. But his impoverished country has become the prey of extortioners, and the resort of banditti of every description; his troops are mutinous; and the nature, or rather confusion of his administration is such, that no command will be obeyed, unless seconded by the presence of armed men. The well-disposed and industrious are not permitted to live undisturbed; cultivation has, in a great degree ceased,—the country has been devastated—the villages burnt,—and food has diminished as thieves and vagrants have accumulated; so that however much Scindiah may be inclined, he has no longer the means of suppressing these disorders. His situation is as little to be envied, as his power is to be dreaded; his authority is confined to the limits of his camp, at Gwalior, and even here he is often exposed to personal insult, from the demands of a seditious army. His government, replete with vice and imbecility, stands on the verge of ruin; his army is reduced to a few battalions of ill-disciplined infantry, with about thirty thousand irregular horse; and there cannot be a doubt, that if left alone, he would soon fall a victim to the power of the Pindarie hordes, whom he has fostered in his bosom. They have, indeed, of late contemned his authority and plundered his provinces; but he submits to these insults, and has hitherto continued to be the protector of a system, which places at his immediate disposal a large body of troops without the expense of maintaining them. He could not, perhaps, have anticipated the height to which the greatness of the Pindaries has lately arisen, and he would now, it may be supposed, gladly reduce their influence; but his ability to do so may be doubted; and it is this which gives cause to apprehend he may be compelled to act a part, contrary to all the dictates of his interest, or in other words, that he may be carried away in a stream which he cannot resist.

In a country where every headman of a village is a petty chief, where there are no established laws, and where the efficiency, or rather existence, of the government depends on the genius and vigour of one man, the death or imbecility of the ruling prince must necessarily plunge his territories into all the horrors of anarchy. Such is at present the condition of the dominions of the late Jeswunt Row Holkar. On the death of this chief, Toolsa Bhye, the mother of the reigning prince, was declared regent during the minority of her son; but the administration of a woman and an infant was not calculated to hold in subjection the rebellious feudatories of a predatory prince. The duties of obedience were consequently soon forgotten, all respect for the head of the government was lost; and while the court was disturbed by the intrigues and turbulence of ambitious men, struggling for power, the army, not content with pillaging their neighbours, turned their swords against each other. The standard of revolt was raised in Candeish, by Bungush Khan, who maintained his authority in that quarter, until his audacity provoked the vengeance of the British Government, who sent a force against him, by which his followers were dispersed and himself taken prisoner.

A great proportion of the troops of Jeswunt Row had, however, attached themselves to the fortunes of Ameer Khan, his favourite general, whose army, in 1807, amounted to about thirty thousand horse, a good train of artillery, and a large body of infantry *. The necessity of providing for the subsistence, and at the same time of indulging the licentious inclinations of his troops, rendered it impossible for Ameer Khan to remain long stationary in any particular spot; and he was, consequently, forced to be incessantly moving from one province to another. In 1809 he invaded the territories of the Rajah of Berar, and would, in all probability, have established himself in the dominions of that prince, had not his ambitious views been foreseen by Lord Minto, then Governor-General. An army, commanded by the late Sir Barry Close, crossed the Nerbudda, in defence of the Rajah of Berar, and compelled the Khan to retire without a battle. This chief, who may be said to be the principal executive officer under the Holkar government, has ever since that period been labouring to secure himself an independence; he has pushed his ravages almost to the borders of the Indus, laid heavy contributions on the Ranas of Joudpoor and Oudipoor, and has lately been employed in the blockade of Jyepoor. His

* MSS.

ascendency appears on the decline, although he possesses a good park of artillery, and a few battalions of bad infantry ; but his horse do not exceed, if they even amount to, ten thousand men. Ameer Khan is a man of ordinary ability, but when young, was active and enterprising ; he is now in the evening of life, and has lost much of his wonted energy and ambition. He seems to have withdrawn from personal attendance at the court of Holkar, whence Toolsa Bhye was driven not long since, by the disputes of the different parties, and unruly conduct of the troops, to throw herself with the young prince on the protection of the Rajah of Kotah. This chief afforded them an asylum; for some months after which, her party having prevailed, she was enabled to return, and revenged herself by torturing and putting many of her enemies to death. These atrocities have rendered her government as unpopular as it was before weak and inefficient ; and, in all probability, we shall not greatly err in predicting its speedy dissolution. Rampoorah *, Chandore, and Galna, are the principal fortresses of the

* A town and district in Ajmere, sixty miles south by east of Jyepoor. Lat. 26° 7′ N., long. 75° 58′ E.

Holkar family. The two latter are in Candeish, and the former in Hindostan.

The extensive province or Soubah of Berar, was formed in the reign of the Emperor Ackbar, and was included in the dominions of the great Mogul, until conquered, as before related, by the Mahratta general Ragojee Bhonslah, in the possession of whose family it has ever since continued. The battle of Argaum was fatal to the prospects, as well as power, of the Rajah of Berar; who, as we have seen, was necessitated to cede, at the peace of 1803, a considerable part of his dependencies to the Company and its allies. He still, however, retained a large tract of territory and several strong fortresses, such as Gawelghur and Narnulla. The dominions of this prince, if we except the woody province of Gundwana; and those districts which are immediately exposed to the destructive irruptions of the Pindaries, are in a higher state of cultivation than most of the other divisions of the Deckan, and produce abundance of wheat, jowarry, and cotton*. His

* The lands of the Jagheerdars, in Berar, are in a more prosperous condition than those of the Circar, because they are better protected, and the ryots less oppressed.

revenues are estimated at forty lacks of rupees annually*; the Rajah maintains eight thousand infantry, a small train of artillery, and about ten thousand ill-mounted horse. The weakness of this state was manifested in its total inability to resist the invasion of Ameer Khan, in 1809; and it has been made still more apparent, by the impunity with which the freebooters of Malwa have impoverished and depopulated many of its most fruitful districts. The degree of suspicion with which the late Rajah had invariably regarded the British Government led him obstinately to reject, even at the hazard of his own existence, our reiterated overtures for a defensive alliance and the establishment of a subsidiary force at Nagpoor. But the death of this prince, which occurred in March, 1816: the imbecility of his son the present Rajah, and the elevation of his nephew Appa Sahib to the regency, have removed these difficulties; and a treaty has been concluded between the two states, on the same basis as those existing between us and the other sovereigns of the Deckan. The mutual benefits likely to result from this alliance will, no doubt, be duly appreciated

* MSS.

by both parties: it will save the subjects of the Rajah from the cruel devastations of sanguinary freebooters; and while it deprives our enemies of the resources of Berar, it affords us a commanding military position, and an easy as well as immediate access into the most vulnerable part of the territory, which has been lately in the occupation of the Pindaries, and will, consequently, facilitate any future operation for the suppression of these robbers.

The principality of Bhopaul, which, from its local situation, and the great efforts it has made to preserve its independence, has lately attracted our attention, was granted by Aurengzebe to a tribe of Patans, of whom the present nabob is a lineal descendant*. It extends north from the Nerbudda, about fifty miles, and is situated between the 77th and 79th degrees of east longitude. It possesses many fertile valleys, but the far greater part of it is mountainous and woody; and for this reason has been selected as an asylum for a body of Pindaries, who have here established themselves, to the utter ruin of the

* MSS.

country and the nabob, whose resources have been reduced from twelve to two lacks of rupees per annum. The soil will produce rice and cotton in abundance, but the cultivation (as is now the case in every other part of Malwa) is confined to the immediate vicinity of fortified places*. Bhopaul, the capital, was once a wealthy and populous town, surrounded by a strong wall and defended by a citadel, but it is now in ruins and almost deserted; the long siege it stood against Scindiah, and the surprising efforts made by its late chief, Vizier Mahomed, in its defence, have however given it great celebrity. The nabob's troops amount to about five hundred infantry and one or two thousand horse, maintained by the Jagheerdars, amongst whom a great part of the province is divided †.

The late nabob Vizier ‡ Mahomed Khan,

* Of these fortifications there are several in Bhopaul; and Goowurghur, a castle on the summit of a hill, about fifteen miles from Hoosingabad, is said to be remarkably strong.

† Previously to the accession of the late Nabob Vizier Mahomed, in 1807, the Rajah of Berar had deprived the Bhopaul state of Hoosingabad, and some other districts in that direction, which have never been recovered.

‡ He died in the spring of 1815.

who was in daily expectation of being overwhelmed by the power of the Mahrattas, had repeatedly and earnestly solicited assistance from the British Government; but the dread of offending Scindiah prevented Lord Minto from receiving * him under our protection. The present nabob has shewn the strongest desire to court our alliance, as the only power that can rescue him from that state of poverty and degradation, to which he has been reduced. The services, rendered by his predecessor to the army under General Goddard, demand our gratitude; his conduct on that occasion drew upon him the indignation and vengeance of Madajee Scindiah, and has never ceased to be remembered by the Mahrattas †. The establishment of a small force in Bhopaul, would be of great advantage to us in the event of war with the predatory powers. The country is naturally strong, and the people, harassed by the continual outrages of the Mahrattas, would exert every nerve to drive these barbarous intruders from

* He entered three years ago into a negotiation with the present Governor-General, which was, however, broken off a few months before his death.—*India Papers.*

† MSS.

the possessions they have usurped. It would give us the command of both banks of the Nerbudda, and completely establish a military line of communication between the armies of Bengal, Madras, and Bombay, through the territories of Berar and Bundelcund.

Our connexion with the Rajahs of Bhurtpoor and Macherry, with the Sikh chiefs between Delhi and the Sutlege, and many others in Hindostan and Bundelcund, has been attended with the most beneficial consequences; they have repaid protection with fidelity, and their countries, instead of suffering from the incursions of the Mahrattas, have enjoyed many years of peace and prosperity. But the rich and fertile plains of Jyenagur (or Jyepoor) once the most populous and flourishing province in Ajmere have, never since the termination of the war in 1806, experienced a moment's repose. The Holkar family have long claimed a right to tribute from the Rajah of Jyepoor; but as such demands are seldom regarded, unless maintained by the presence of an army, Ameer Khan, as the general of Holkar, has, under pretence of collecting this tribute, brought desolation on every part of the

Rajah's territories. That prince has for several years past sustained a siege in his capital; his revenues have been exhausted, and he has at length, by the sale of his jewels, been enabled to purchase a transitory respite from his miseries. The hatred which this prince bears the predatory powers is hereditary; his recent injuries must have imbittered that sentiment, and although he may feel dissatisfied with our former treatment * of him, he must ever look towards us for support. The friendship of this chieftain ought to be cultivated; his territories are extensive, and not only contiguous to ours, but it is through them that an enemy from Malwa must march to the attack of the upper provinces of Hindostan. The Rajah has of late suffered many severe losses, but he could still assist us with a body of irregular horse, and with the resources of his country. But before this can be accomplished, we must guarantee his safety from the future attacks of his enemies, a measure calculated equally to promote our honour and our interests.

Amongst the many petty princes of Raj-

---

* Vide Malcolm's Political History of India.

pootana, no one has rendered himself more deservedly conspicuous or more universally respected, than Zalim Sing, the usurping* chief of Kotah. The acknowledged ability and prudence of this chief, joined to the centrical position of his territory which extends along the east bank of the Chumbul, has given him a degree of consequence amongst the contending factions of Hindostan, that occasions his friendship and alliance to be courted by all parties. He has twice afforded protection to the Holkar family; once when Jeswant Row fled before the British army, and some months ago, when Toolsa Bhye and her infant son were driven from Indore by the seditious soldiery. The district of Kotah is said to yield a revenue of about thirty lacks of rupees†; the Rajah has in his employ a small body of infantry, and between three and four thousand good horse; his country is hilly, difficult of access, and full of intricate passes. Zalim Sing is at this moment intimately connected with Ameer Khan, but there cannot be a doubt that he

* He has ever since 1805 kept his master the Rajah in confinement.

† MSS.

would gladly exchange the uncertain friendship of a freebooter, for the alliance of a great power which could relieve him from the danger, with which he is hourly threatened by the lawless tribes in his vicinity.

Joudpoor is the largest of the Rajpoot states, but the power of Maun Sing, the reigning prince, is not equal to his extent of territory, which approaches the Indus on one side, and touches Jyenagar on the other. He has never been able to resist the ravages of the Mahrattas, to whom this state has paid tribute for more than half a century. The present disorganized state of the governments of Scindiah and Holkar might materially contribute towards the increase of his influence and security, had he not fallen into the hands of a bolder and more cruel plunderer, Ameer Khan; who, with the greatest part of his army, may be said to have subsisted, for many years past, upon the resources of this prince. The dominions of Maun Sing are divided amongst numerous Jagheerdars, who hold their lands on condition of supporting a certain number of troops for the service of their prince in time of war; but as these lands are transmitted from father to son, the terms of the tenure are forgotten, or the government is unable to enforce them; and the majority of the Jagheerdars can, therefore, only be regarded as petty usurpers.

The Rajah of Mewar or Oudipoor, sometimes denominated the Rana of Chitore, is the representative of the most ancient and illustrious family in Hindostan *. It is deemed an honour to be allied with him, and the ardour with which the hands of the different Princesses of Chitore have been sought by the neighbouring princes, has, on more than one occasion, deluged the adjoining countries in blood. The principality of Oudipoor is about a hundred miles in length by eighty in breadth, and runs along the south-east border of Joudpoor. The country is strong, mountainous, and fertile; in part divided amongst a number of feudal lords, and in part occupied by the Mahrattas, whose pernicious influence has greatly diminished the power of the Rana †. The subjects of this prince, as well as those of the Rajah of Joudpoor, are

* This family is also said to be descended from the famous Nushirvan.

† His authority may be said to be confined to the town and valley of Oudipoor.

of the Rajpoot caste, high-spirited and brave to excess, impatient of restraint, but at the same time peaceful, indolent, and desirous of being left unmolested by their neighbours. The Rajpoot states of Ajmere contain the only vestiges of the ancient Hindoo government of India; they defended their rights and their religion with unexampled courage against the Mahomedans, and if we are even compelled to war with the predatory states of Malwa, we could not adopt a safer or better line of policy than that of extending their authority at the expense of the Mahrattas. These princes would be to our Government the best of dependent allies; their condition would be that to which they have ever been habituated, and paying a fixed but moderate tribute, their countries would become rich and flourishing under our protection.

I have failed in my efforts to acquire very correct information regarding the movements of Runjut Sing, the chief of Lahore. He is, however, still in arms, and has long threatened the invasion of Cashmere and Moultan.

CHAP. VII.

It may be thought that I have drawn an exaggerated picture of the aspect of affairs in India; but so far from having overcharged, I have but faintly and imperfectly described the disorders which at this moment prevail. The truth is, that no native government can long exist in collision with a state, regulated on such principles as the British empire in India; and if we are doomed, as many think, to be lost in expansion, we are fast approaching the verge of ruin, since the territories of our allies must imperceptibly fall into our hands, whilst those of Holkar and Scindiah, if left to themselves, will daily become more and more a chaos of discord, alike calculated to produce the elements of internal misery and foreign danger. The powerful arm of the British Government can alone arrest the progress of these disorders; and although it must be admitted that our possessions are sufficiently extensive, yet it becomes a question, alike interesting and important, whether it would not be more easy for us to maintain our ascendency in the East, by granting to an industrious race the relief and full benefit of our laws, than by supporting the ministers of weak and vicious princes, in acts of habitual aggression upon their own subjects? The Hindoos, who form the mass of the population of India, are in general brave and tenacious of ancient customs, but proverbially docile and industrious; and numbers who have been forced by the barbarous rulers under whom they live, or by whom they are surrounded, to quit the plough for the sword, might easily be induced to resume their former occupations. Humanity (if such a term can find a place in diplomacy), as well as policy, imperatively demand our speedy and determined interposition: the period has arrived when neutrality is impracticable, and it is for higher authority to devise the best mode of restoring the violated peace and tranquillity of India. With a nation, like the Mahrattas, we can never be respected when we cease to be dreaded: the experience of years has shewn us the inefficiency and ruinous absurdity of a defensive system; our extensive lines are of no avail, they provoke rather than repress the daring spirit of our enemies, whose flying parties of horse have passed through the midst of our armies, and devastated with impunity, the naked and defenceless provinces in their rear. The Mahrattas, it is said, begin to entertain a notion, that we are to be conquered by a desultory warfare, and that the incessant attack of great bodies of horse, while they carefully avoid a general action with our troops, will ruin our resources, unhinge the allegiance of our subjects, shake the doubtful fidelity of our allies, and remove the impression which is generally entertained of our resistless superiority.

From a defensive system we have every thing to dread and nothing to hope, we are dishonoured in the eyes of our subjects, and in those of our allies; we are put to an enormous and indefinite expense, our armies are harassed and worn out by long and toilsome marches in pursuit of an enemy, whom they can seldom overtake, while the Pindaries, joined in their march by all the idle and discontented, swell as they continue to advance*. At such a crisis we are not only justified, but it becomes our paramount duty to make use of all the power which we possess; it is a duty which we owe to ourselves, to our injured and suffering subjects, and to the millions of our fellow-creatures, whose happiness or misery hangs upon the line of policy we resolve to pursue. No moment could be more propitious for any great undertaking than the present; we have nothing to fear from foreign invasion, our late successes in Nepaul and at Hatrass have raised our reputation, and damped the confidence of our enemies, while our armies were never so formidable, nor more conveniently posted for immediate action. We ought, therefore, to avail ourselves of these advantages for a complete revision of our political system, and the adoption of a general arrangement, at once calculated to secure the stability of our power, and to secure the peace of India on a broad and lasting basis.

If our efforts are to be limited to the mere

* The party of Pindaries, which lately ravaged Ganjam, consisted of one thousand five hundred horse, when they passed the Nerbudda; but their numbers had increased to five thousand when they entered the Company's territory.

suppression of the Pindaries, the nature of our operations must, of course, in a great measure depend on the proceedings of the principal predatory powers, or in other words, Dowlut Row Scindiah, Holkar, and Ameer Khan. These chiefs are, in fact, so blended with the Pindaries, that it would be scarcely possible to make war upon one without becoming involved in hostilities with the others; but if Scindiah, Holkar, and Ameer Khan could be prevailed upon to aid us in our plans for the suppression of these banditti, the task would be comparatively easy. I fear, however, that it is vain to expect any thing like an efficient or cordial co-operation on the part of these chiefs; it would be requiring of them at once to abandon the ideas that have been instilled into them from their earliest youth, to destroy the common bond of union between their adherents; and to abjure the very spirit and essence of their institutions. A Mahratta is the child of rapine, his education incapacitates him from appreciating the blessings of social order; and he looks with the same horror on a life of industry, as the pacific boor of another country would contemplate that in which he so much delights.

Overtures will, no doubt, be made to those chiefs, and they will be called upon to declare their intentions, and to avow the line they mean to take; since in a contest like the present, we cannot admit of neutrality. It is frivolous to talk of a strict observance of our treaties with Scindiah and Holkar; the conduct of the former has long since virtually annulled the treaty of 1806, and the government of Holkar expired with that chief. We may conclude from the whole tenor of Scindiah's late proceedings, that he either has not the power, or wants the inclination to check the progress of the Pindaries; he has hitherto evaded all our demands for their suppression, and it cannot be denied, that under cover of their name, he has carried on war against us and our allies, for these several years past. He is surrounded by men of abandoned principles, and a licentious army over whom he has little or no control. Several of the former are known to be in the interest of the Pindarie chiefs, while there are the strongest grounds to conclude, that parties of the latter not unfrequently accompany these freebooters in their inroads into our territories.

The dread of approaching danger might,

perhaps, alarm Scindiah, and incline him to listen to our proposals ; but if we are to judge from past events, and the sentiments which this chieftain has never ceased to entertain towards us, little dependence can be placed on professions extorted by fear. A reluctant or forced acquiescence, in the propositions made to him, would probably be accompanied by secret endeavours to counteract our views, and prove more detrimental to the success of the general cause, than an open and avowed hostility. Should Scindiah, however, contrary to expectation, zealously enter into our plans, his aid and influence would, no doubt, most essentially contribute towards the destruction of the Pindaries.

Proposals of friendship will, no doubt, be made to the widow regent, or representative of the house of Holkar, and it may be policy in us to take the young prince under our protection ; and, if possible, support his authority in such a manner as to establish some form of government, that would prevent his country from continuing, as at present, an asylum for the Pindaries, a great proportion of whom may be said to subsist upon its resources.

Should, however, all our endeavours to secure the co-operation of the predatory powers prove futile, it might, in my opinion, be regarded rather as a fortunate occurrence than otherwise; since it would enable us to carry our plans for the future peace of India more completely into effect. The great extent and mountainous nature of the country they at present occupy, their jarring interests and perpetual feuds, would render any thing like a general combination or confederacy against us totally impracticable; and even were their whole power united, it would be incapable of resisting the overwhelming force we have collected on their frontier. Our armies surround them in almost every direction in Hindostan, in Bundelcund, in Berar, in the Deckan, and in Guzzerat, and only wait for orders to attack them in every quarter. Their strong holds, their families, and their treasures, would successively fall into our hands. The only fear we can entertain is, that they would not venture to meet us in action, their troops would disperse, and we should, in all probability, find ourselves involved in a long and toilsome contest with an enemy that was almost intangible. But the war, though protracted, would be final; and the countries which we aided, would furnish us with ample means to complete the reduction of our enemies; as we should, probably, find in the revival of the authority of the native Hindoo princes, the best of all securities against the re-appearance of their oppressors *.

The Mahratta power has never been fixed on any solid basis in Hindostan; it is still regarded as an intruder in Malwa, and its expulsion would be at once easy of achievement and beneficial to a country, to the prosperity and happiness of which its rule has been so baneful. This is, in all probability, the last war in which we shall be involved for many years; its successful issue will leave us the undisputed masters of the vast peninsula of India, and we shall have to decide upon the future destinies of seventy millions of

* The excellency of the policy lately adopted by the Governor-General, in the employment of numerous bodies of irregular horse, cannot be sufficiently commended. It must be attended with the most beneficial effects; it will increase our means of offence in the most necessary arm, add greatly to our popularity, and provide for the subsistence of thousands, who might otherwise be compelled to swell the ranks of our enemies.

souls. If compelled to a policy that places us in this situation, we shall have to consider whether we are to receive the whole or any part of the countries we may conquer under our own immediate management, or whether parts of them shall be restored, under certain conditions and restrictions, to Scindiah and Holkar; or be divided amongst those of our allies, who may assist us in the prosecution of the war; or restored to the ancient families of the country, on conditions that may place them in subjection to our power.

If the events which I have anticipated should take place, I should deprecate the idea of any part of Malwa being restored to predatory chiefs, because no reliance can be placed on their friendship; and we should always be exposed, in a greater or less degree, to the same dangers as those under which we now labour. We should either be compelled to exercise an invidious interference in all their internal arrangements, or the territories restored to them would soon relapse into the same chaos of confusion, from which we suppose it to have been redeemed. At the same time it would be neither politic nor desirable that we should ourselves immediately occupy any part of this exhausted province; nor is it to be supposed, the Government in England would readily sanction the extension of our territory in this quarter. A part of Malwa might be given to the Rajah of Berar; the principality of Bhopaul might be enlarged, and a very considerable proportion of the conquered countries divided between the Rajpoot princes, on whose friendship we might rely with perfect confidence, and under whose management, with occasional aid and advice from us, the territories under their rule, would rapidly improve. In conformity with the principles which have been already adopted, our allies should severally be made to retain a quota of troops for the preservation of tranquillity in their respective possessions; and in this manner subsistence and employment would be found for numbers of the military classes, who would be recovered from their idle and profligate pursuits by the gradual operation of a settled system, and a judicious mixture of mildness and severity. It is certainly our policy to avoid, as far as we can with safety, the increase of our territory. Our dominions on the west coast of India ought, however, to be connected with those in Bundelcund; and, with this object, the possessions of Holkar and Scindiah, in Candeish, would for many reasons be a most valuable acquisition. These are not, however, the only arrangements we should have to consider; we must direct our attention once more to the Peishwah and the Nizam, and more particularly to the latter. I have already dwelt at great length on the evils arising out of the nature of our present connexion with the Nizam; but I am by no means aware that the evils of which we complain would be in any degree lessened, were we to withdraw from all interference in his concerns, whereas the resources of his country might, in that event, be turned against us. We have, therefore, only a choice of difficulties; and the question may be considered as one of the most serious and embarrassing, on which we can be called upon to decide in the government of this great and extraordinary empire.

I have stated freely my opinions, but these are not, perhaps, entitled to much consideration; they are formed at a distance from the scene of action, and without the means of acquiring that accurate information which was necessary to enable me to discuss a subject of such importance. I may, however, be allowed to express my confidence, founded on the experience of past measures, that nothing will be left undone, which wisdom or energy can accomplish, by the illustrious person now at the head of our Indian Government.

THE END.